The Outlaw of Megantic

Bernard Epps

The Outlaw of Megantic

M&S

FOR SUSAN

© 1973 by Bernard Epps

Reprinted 1988

Annotated section for classroom use by Peter Peart
Translations from the Gaelic by Rhoda MacRitchie and
Ann Leckie.

CANADIAN CATALOGUING PUBLICATION DATA

Epps, Bernard, 1936-
    The outlaw of Megantic

"This special edition for schools includes an additional
section with ideas for classroom activities, notes and
questions."

ISBN 0-7710-3102-5

I. Morrison, Donald, 1858-1894 – Fiction.
I. Title.

PS8509.P67098   C813'.5'4   C74-3341-7
PR9199.3.E66098

Manufactured in Canada by Webcom Limited

McClelland and Stewart
The Canadian Publishers
481 University Avenue
Toronto, Ontario
M5G 2E9

Soiridh leis gach beinn 'us fireach
  A' bheinn o'm mithich dhomh 'bhi triall,
Guidheam fada féidh a'd ghlacaibh;
  B'e bhi'n taice riut mo mhiann.

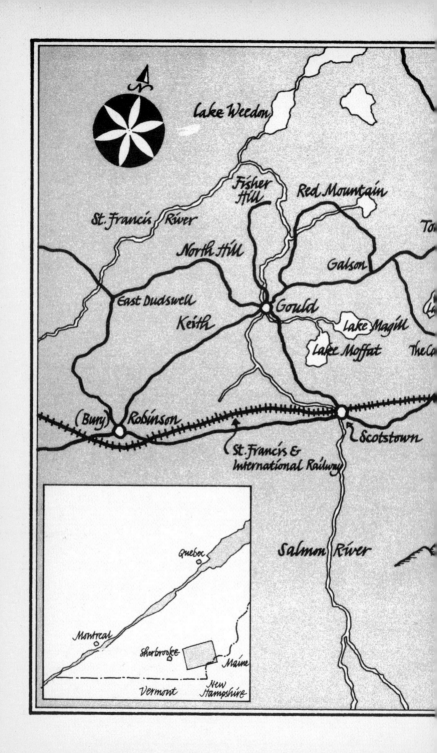

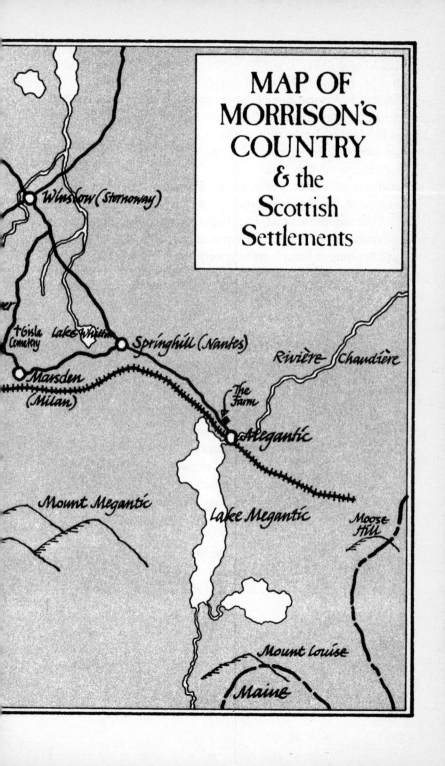

MAP OF
MORRISON'S
COUNTRY
& the
Scottish
Settlements

Winslow (Stornoway)

+Gisla
Cemetery   Lake Whitton

Springhill (Nantes)

Rivière   Chaudière

Marsden
(Milan)

The
Farm

Megantic

Mount Megantic

Lake Megantic

Moose
Hill

Mount Louise

Maine

Foreword

In the following tale, I have tried to keep faith, not only with the facts, but with the legend of Donald Morrison. That legend has survived almost a century and is vigorous yet among the people of Compton County, and it is in deference to this vigour that I have employed the techniques of fiction. His bones lie in a small neglected cemetery but his myth walks yet among the people.

This legend, in fact, has proved more enduring than the country. Many of the settlements mentioned in this book are no longer found on any map and others have entirely changed both name and character. Marsden is now Milan. Spring Hill has become Nantes. Winslow is called Stornoway and all that survives of Dudswell is in St-Adolphe-de-Dudswell.

There have been two books to date on Donald Morrison. The first, *Donald Morrison; The Canadian Outlaw*, was written entirely in verse by Oscar Dhu, the "Lingwick Bard," and published in 1892 while Donald still lay in prison. The second, *Donald Morrison; the Megantic Outlaw*, by Henry G. Kidd, was privately printed in 1948. Neither made use of contemporary documents – newspaper accounts or courthouse records – and both altered, or carefully avoided, the names of certain protagonists. Donald's story is far better than has yet been told, better even than legend remembers, and time enough has passed to make delicacy inexcusable.

My thanks are due to Donald Morrison, Scotstown, namesake of this legend's hero, who dug from his collection old books I would not otherwise have found.

BERNARD EPPS
Lindisfarne
May 1972

Part One

Major Malcolm B. McAulay

In the village of Megantic, in the county of Compton, in the province of Quebec, in the year 1885, there was a dispute over the terms of a mortgage.

Major Malcolm B. McAulay, money-lender of that village, was seated at a large roll-top desk in his office and entering receipts into a ledger.

"Good morning, Major McAulay."

"And a good day to yourself, Donald Morrison."

Donald Morrison, farmer, ex-cowboy, speaking on behalf of his father, had come to put matters on a personal basis.

"It is a fine spring we are having."

"It is that and so it is. What can I be doing for you?"

McAulay was a very busy man.

"I have some business to be talking."

"I am listening, then."

But the major turned his attention again to his books and turned his back to Donald. Donald sat down on a wooden chair, turned his hat in his hands, licked his lips, blinked his eyes and then jumped up, strode forward and leaned on the edge of the desk where he could at least look down at the back of the major's neck.

"It's about that mortgage on our place," he began softly. "There's been a mistake somewhere."

"Oh?"

McAulay turned a page and began totting a column of figures. Donald's jaw hardened.

"My father was owing me a bit of money. He took a mortgage on the place to be paying it off but he was somehow getting less than half the money he was supposed to."

"Oh?"

He made three syllables of it but went on with his work.

"You arranged it that way, McAulay."

Donald's tone brought the major's face up quickly and they eyed each other.

"And why should I be doing that, sir?"

"I said it was a mistake."

"There was no mistake on my part, sir. If your father did not understand the terms of the agreement, that was *his* mistake, sir. Not mine."

"My father may not read nor write too well but the man can count. You cheated him."

The major's face turned scarlet. He offered to throw Donald bodily down the stairs and was invited promptly to try it. The major offered to have him arrested. The cowboy made a counter-offer, which was to show the major his pistols, to push both barrels up the major's nose and blow the major's ears off.

Discussion faltered at that and each man stared furiously at the other as tempers slowly subsided. The major turned back to his ledger and began totting the column a second time. Donald remained where he was and studied the small hairs on the back of the major's neck.

"There was a ninety-day promissary note included in the mortgage," said Donald at last and quietly. "It was for four hundred dollars. On the bottom margin is a note which says 'To be credited on the principal when called.' That means you never really hand over the money."

The major's voice was loud and strained.

"It is all strictly legal, sir."

He lost his place in his passion and began the column a third time.

"My father never would have agreed to that if he'd been

understanding it," Donald continued in the same sub-
dued voice. "You were taking advantage of the fact that
he reads or writes no English. You were knowing he did
not understand."

"That mortgage was and is perfectly legal, sir."

He began totting his figures for yet a fourth time and
Donald suddenly slammed the flat of his hand on the desk
and roared at the man.

"Look at me when I'm talking to you!"

The major started at this explosion and glanced up
aghast. He wasn't used to being spoken to in this fashion
and he didn't like it. He did not like it at all. His thick
brows met in fury.

"Either you meet the exact terms of that mortgage, sir,
or you vacate the property! Is that clear?"

"It is clear that you are a miserly grasping old crocodile."

"Get out of my office, sir! Get out!"

"A black-hearted cheat and a swindler!"

"Get out before I have the police on you!"

"A greedy, miserable, rancid . . ."

"Get out, I say!"

". . . foul-smelling sack of pig shit!"

But as soon as he was back on the street in the fresh
breeze from the lake, Donald knew he had muffed it. He
had come to speak reasonably with the man, to be cold and
calculating, to talk business and work out some arrangement satisfactory to all concerned but his passion had got
the better of his resolutions and he had muffed it. The
farm was in more peril now than it had been before and
the only recourse left was the Courts of Law.

Murdo Morrison

It was a good farm. It stood on a hilltop a mile and three-quarters north of the village of Megantic, east of the Springhill Road, and commanded a grand view of the lake, the mountains, the surrounding forests. It contained one hundred acres, two good barns and a fine house. Murdo and his sons had hacked the farm from the wilderness, torn out the stumps, ripped up the stones, raised fences and buildings and fertilized every foot of the land with blood, sweat and pain.

Donald was Murdo's youngest. He had gone for a cowboy in the North-West Territories in 1879 when he was twenty-one. With Norman McAulay, a friend from the Middle District, he had ridden all over the western ranges, learned to rope and to shoot with deadly accuracy. When his father sent for him four years later, Donald came home to the Scottish settlements in the hills of Quebec, paid off the old man's debts and managed the farm for almost two years. To repay him something for his money and his labour, Murdo had taken a first mortgage with Major McAulay. McAulay's first rule of business was to keep his purse on a string – like a schoolboy playing tricks on the passers-by – jerking it home as soon as it was touched, and this left old Murdo broke and bewildered after the agreement where he was simply broke before.

He was bewildered now as he sat in his socks at the kitchen table with papers spread out in the lamplight. His bald head was bowed to the lamp and Donald could see a crease around his forehead where the old man's hat habitually rested – a crease like the trench-line at a battlefront. Up to that furrow, the face was brown and weathered and wrinkled as an old elm. Beyond, the skin stretched thin, smooth, white, startlingly vulnerable.

"We'll just have to take McAulay to court," said Donald. "We can't be letting him take the farm."

"Ach," said old Murdo, "I've no liking at all for legal humbug."

He passed a huge old hand over his pate and worried the papers trying to make some sense of it all, trying to wrench some meaning from the shapes of letters and patterns of words that might as well have been Old Egyptian for all of him. He was a hard man, an honest man, tough, stern and determined, but he had no head at all for the convolutions and careful hedging of legal business. He still believed a man's word was his law and all writing outside the scriptures was so much hokum. Donald knew that times had changed and the courts took an opposite view – man's word was hokum and his writings scripture.

"Maybe if I'm going down to talk with the man . . ." said old Murdo, painfully, but he lacked words to finish the thought.

"It's only lawyers he'll listen to now," Donald said. "I'll be hiring one in the morning."

He gathered up the papers and took them with him the next morning. It was all amazingly complicated to his eye but the lawyer seemed to have no trouble sorting things out. He read them through quickly, asked a few pertinent questions and announced that Donald had a very good case. They would overturn the mortgage as fraudulent and if Donald would just leave a small retainer for immediate expenses, he would begin fashioning the suit immediately.

"It's purely a technicality," he said. "Purely a technicality, I do assure you."

His name was McLean – Donald had intentionally sought out a fellow Scot – and he was a round-faced little man with a bland smile and an air of harried urgency. He spoke of law courts with an affectionate contempt and created the impression that they were bank vaults to which he had the combination. He spoke of the thousands he had made for other clients and, although Donald was rather uneasy at hiring a safe-cracker rather than an advocate, the man was so blissfully confident, so ready and eager to serve that Donald retained him to press the suit and returned home in a more cheerful frame of mind.

He found his father picking stones from a freshly plowed field so he could get on with the harrowing and planting. No matter how long the land had been cultivated, no matter how many rocks were dug out, picked up and hauled to the edge of the field, the earth was such that there were always more to be gathered each spring as the first hard crop of the year. The earth was fruitful of stones. They multiplied themselves beneath the snows, pushed up as the frost went down and grew huge in the sunshine.

The old man straightened from prying a great stone from its roots, took off his hat and mopped his bald head with a grubby red cloth. His joints seemed to be rustier this spring and the rocks more stubborn, but Murdo could still match anything in God's creation for stubbornness. The old horse tossed his mane at the stone-boat and Murdo saw his son coming across the field with his jacket slung over his shoulder.

"How did it go then, Donald?" asked Murdo as he replaced his hat precisely in its crease.

"'Well enough," said Donald. "They say we've a good case and there's nothing to be worrying on."

He measured the stone with his eyes, laid his coat on the earth and slowly rolled up his sleeves.

"You'll be taking McAulay to court, then?"

"We will," said Donald.

The old man shook his head and spat. "I've no liking for this legal business," he said. "No liking at all."

"We can't be letting him take the farm," said Donald. "I don't care what anybody says, McAulay's not getting this farm."

He bent down, set his feet, put his shoulder to the stone and his hands underneath, took hold and heaved. The boulder rolled smoothly onto the stone-boat and came to rest. Murdo looked sourly at his son.

"You've got yourself soiled," he said. He shoved his grimy handkerchief back into his pocket, tossed the pry-bar on the boat and gathered the reins. "Go get yourself changed and you can be helping me finish."

"I thought I might be going up to see Augusta," said Donald, squinting rather shyly at his stern old father. He brushed dirt from his sleeves and rolled them down. "Since I'm all dressed up anyway."

Murdo nodded. "As you like then," he said, and clucked the horse into motion. Donald picked up his coat and watched his father to the edge of the field. He didn't expect praise but a friendly word once in a while would not go amiss. His father was getting too old for that sort of work, too, but there was no way of getting him to take things easy. He was a stubborn old devil and no mistake. He'd do himself an injury lifting those great rocks one of these years but his work was his pride and you can't take pride away from any man. Donald watched as the boulder was added to the thousands already picked and stored at the fenceline over the years and headed for the road. They looked like they were all on display and awaiting a customer. If there was sale for rocks, he thought, then all these stubborn old Scots would be millionaires.

Augusta McIver

It was thirteen miles to Marsden where Augusta lived with her parents, but Donald enjoyed the walk. He enjoyed the chance to stretch his legs among the hills and trees of home again after so many years in the parched flatlands of the North-West. Mount Megantic loomed on his left and Saint Sebastian on his right and straight ahead, at Spring Hill, was a halfway house called Finlay's Tavern where he could stop to oil his throat and chat with the customers. It was good to be home again.

It was a good country to call home, too. The houses were scattered and the villages few and all the rest was booming forest and leaping rivers, quiet lakes and steaming swamps. On a far-off ridge, a clearing showed where a road went through and the settlers had hacked down the shade beside it to build their farms. It was like sowing peas when the first settlers came in. They were brought out in waggons and dropped off at each side of the road — one here, one there, the next across the way — like sowing peas. Each man had gone into the trees and begun laying about him with an axe — week after week, month after month, year after year.

And when the shade was down, piled up and burned away, there were stumps and stones to be uprooted, cabins to build, barns and fences and children to make. It was a hard life but a good one and if a man were just stubborn enough, he might eventually find himself proprietor of a few cleared acres, a few pigs, chickens, sheep and cattle, a good house, a barn and a carriage shed, a fine team in front of a buggy in summer and a sleigh in winter — a rich harvest for his years. A man could be his own, then, beholden to none. He could speak the Gaelic among his friends, raise his family straight and strong and not a soul in the world could tell him what to do.

That was what settled the country when you came right down to it: your backside to the nay-sayers and the chance at independence. The laird at home on Lewis had wanted sheep and sent the crofters packing. What fish and game there were belonged to him as so much cattle and he often took more thought for his grouse, his salmon and his deer than he did for his people. The people had turned their backsides at him, then, and came where there were no landlords, where fish and game belonged equally to all and a man could be his own.

If he were lucky enough to stay clear of the money-lenders, that is. There was always that. For fifty years there had not even been a bank east of Eaton and debts were paid in kind, but with the railroad and civilization came the money-lenders.

He was at Spring Hill almost before he knew it, and stepped out of the sun into the welcome of Finlay McLeod's hotel. The Matheson brothers, Willie and Pete, were at a table arguing as usual with Mac McLean for referee. Mac was the section boss on the railway. Peter Matheson worked with him and Willie was the local blacksmith — and possibly the single dirtiest man in all the Townships. He managed to be always black with axle grease and the soot from his forge from ten minutes after church was out on Sunday to ten minutes before the next service. He always managed a three-day beard and carried the stub of a homemade cigarette in his mouth but, in spite of his grime and his gruffness, Willie was known as one of the best-hearted men in the country.

They greeted Donald with shouts and insults, slaps on the back and digs in the ribs, and ordered Finlay to hop-to with a fresh round of drinks. Donald sat down and gladly told a few tales of his cowboying days. Finlay joined them. They wanted to know if Donald had his pistols with him and if he was as good a shot as everyone said. He admitted he was carrying his guns but declined to exhibit them. Willie maintained that Donald could hit a mark equally well with his left as with his right hand, which prompted Peter to doubting it vehemently. They took opposing views on every question as a matter of course and argued each stand fiercely. Bets were offered and accepted and nothing would do but they all had to step outside for a demonstration. Finlay offered his wife's clotheslines for targets. Donald protested. They insisted. He drew both guns at once, cut one with a bullet from his right, the other with a bullet from his left hand gun. Finlay's red-flannels fluttered to the grass.

The shots brought Mrs. McLeod out like a shrill black fury. She saw her linen on the grass and lay about her with the rough edge of her tongue until Donald, the Mathesons and Mac McLean split up and fled for their lives, leaving poor Finlay alone to face her music.

Donald walked cheerfully on to Marsden and was guided on the last fifty yards by the intriguing smell of barley bread from the McIver kitchen. The door stood open to let out the heat of the baking and Donald walked softly in.

Augusta — slim, dark, nineteen — laboured over the stove with her sleeves rolled and a damp curl of hair against her cheek. Donald pulled loose the bow of her apron. She swung round, saw him standing so close and squealed. He grinned. She blushed red as a poppy, swiped at her hair, wrung her hands on her apron, made a more respectable distance between them and averted her face. She looked desperately left and right for something to do and began wiping the table clean.

"**Dad**'s in the fields," she said, "if you're wanting to see him."

"It's you I've come to visit," he announced and the man walked right over, **bold** as you please, turned a chair and sat himself down astride. You'd think he owned the place, he was that comfortable. And the house in a mess and she in her dreadful old skirt and carpet slippers! The least the man could have done was give a girl a bit of a warning instead of marching right in and sitting there watching her with a smile spread all over his great face.

"Well, then," said she, still a-fluster and trying to tuck back that annoying lock of hair and re-tie her apron strings all at once, "if you've walked all the way from the Lake this day, you'll be wanting a cup of tea."

"I will," said he, still grinning, "and a bit of that fresh barley bread. It's been making my teeth water these last five miles."

Just like he owned the place! Sitting there in his great boots, ordering up his *strupach*, grinning like a baboon and not giving a girl the breath of a chance to get trim and tidied in case — just in case, mind — in case he might be wanting to ask her out or something later.

There was nothing for it. She served up his tea with small-talk and bread still warm from the oven and a bit of new-made butter to be spreading on it while avoiding as much as possible his amused and admiring eyes. Her mother came bouncing up from the cellar with the supper potatoes and made things worse by clucking with pleasure and fussing over him like a mother hen. Anyone would think it was she the man had come to visit. She laughed at everything he said, twinkled and winked and licked her lips over him as if he were a pudding. Her father stamped in with a hearty hello and a glad handshake for the man and Augusta took the opportunity to flee upstairs.

She combed out her dark hair, parted it carefully in the centre and got it put back behind her neck with a cameo of Queen Victoria. She freshened her face and spent an agonizing time choosing clothes. She didn't want to be too dressed up for fear the man would think she did it only for him but yet she wanted to look her best. She wanted him thinking this was the way she usually freshened up of an evening after a hard day over a hot stove but she wanted above all to draw no remarks from her father about being all dressed up like a dish of fish. She settled on a white blouse and a black skirt — simple and clean and neat. She changed her shoes, studied herself in the glass, decided she was a trifle too plain and added a small locket from her box. It was just another visit from just another neighbour, she told herself, and went back downstairs.

Her father, meanwhile, had hauled Donald up by the sleeve and over to the woodbox. "Hist, now," he said, "for I've a wee jug of the creature hidden away here." He winked at Donald and cast an elaborate glance over his shoulder to see if the women were back. He quickly fished up the bottle, uncorked it and shoved it at Donald. "Here. Take a good swaller. Quick, now. Have a good one. Quick!" He glanced once more towards the kitchen door as Donald put the bottle to his lips and did his duty. "That's enough, now. No sense in making a pig of yourself!" He took a quick snort in his own right, sighed, corked up, wiped his chin on his sleeve, glanced guiltily about once more and returned the bottle to its nest behind the woodbox.

They were back at the table angelically innocent when Augusta came in. She smiled at Donald in a neighbourly way and looked quickly off before he could give her his grin. It was obvious what the pair had been up to behind her back — fancy hiding a bottle where anyone standing over the stove could see it with only half an eye! — but she pretended not to know for fear of spoiling their fun. If they wanted to act like small boys smoking behind the schoolhouse, it was none of her concern.

Her mother came in with the meat and they got the dinner going. She smiled briefly at the locket her daughter wore but said no word and even her father, thank the Lord, made no teasing comment to redden her cheeks. He and Donald had their heads together and were talking of sheep, of cattle and seed, and she had to set the table about their elbows. She got out the cakes and scones and made another good pot of tea and began to feel she might yet survive this visit.

After supper was done, after news and gossip and general tittle-tattle were all exchanged, then Mac McLean came in with his pipes and his wife and little John McLeod showed up with his harmonica. Her father got out his fiddle and they had a bit of a *ceilidh*. Donald was pressed for a song. McLean play a *pibroch* on his bag of wind and her father leapt to the fray like an old war-horse and contributed the crazy stamping dance he'd learned from the French. There was nothing he loved better than a fair chance to make a fool of himself in public. Augusta sat with her hands in her lap and a smile on her lips and Donald was watching her even when he was looking the other way.

And then, just when everything was going fine, what did her father do but whisper to John and wink at Mac and start up "Ho ro, My Nut-Brown Maiden." Mrs. McLean laughed like a duck, her mother smiled and they all joined in and sang it straight at her until she thought the flush of blood in her cheeks would fry them crisp as bacon.

> "Ho ró, mo nighean donn, bhòidheach,
>   Hi ri, mo nighean donn, bhòidheach,
> Mo chaileag laghach, bhòidheach,
> Cha phòsainn ach thu."

Aye, she was that embarrassed she could have crawled under the lounge like a mouse and died there in the dark but she'd be hanged if she'd ever give any of them the satisfaction and so she sat it all through like a prisoner in the dock and even stared straight at Donald once or twice and didn't go out to make more tea until they were well into the middle of "Praise of Islay."

But who do you think followed her out to the kitchen but Donald himself!

"Augusta," he said, soft as silk and bold as you please, "I've got something to be asking you."

Her heart did a wild stamping dance of its own and she spilled some of the tea from the pot to the floor.

"Yes?" said she, calm as she could.

She looked up into the laughing blue eyes of the man. Her mouth was dry as old leaves.

"But it will have to wait," he said.

She wanted to throw the pot at his head, kick him in the shins, pull out that great cheeky moustache of his and . . . and . . . but he was no longer smiling. His face was serious and a trifle worried. He touched her arm.

"Just a week or two until I'm getting some business cleared up," he said. "Then I'll come round and ask it. That's a promise."

And without another word, leaving her holding the tea-pot in one hand and the place on her arm with the other like some great gillie-gaupus, the man got into his coat and slipped out the door.

Mr. McLean

The little round-faced lawyer came up with a scheme to force the farm to sheriff's sale, and thereby establish a legal market value, relieve old Murdo of all responsibilities and simplify the matter of overturning the mortgage afterwards. Donald immediately protested that he did not want the farm sold, that he was trying his damndest to hang on to it. McLean smiled at his ignorance.

"It's purely a technicality," he said. "I do assure you."

Donald failed to understand.

"You have only to buy it at auction," said McLean, "for a nominal sum and you will be free, as the sole owner of the property, to pursue the case unencumbered."

"But I've no money to buy the place," protested Donald and again the little man smiled with blissful confidence.

"Money — actual cash — will not be necessary," he said. "It's purely a technicality."

"But the mortgage, then. The mortgage is with my father and not with me."

"Exactly. We must close with McAulay and do battle directly. He, of course, is technically the real owner of the property. He will oppose the sale but there'll be nothing he can do to prevent it and the only way he can still make a profit on his investment, is to let the mortgage run on — merely transferring it to your name. Once he has done that, he has fallen right into our trap."

He rubbed his hands together and smiled with pleasure at his own cleverness, but Donald still failed to applaud. He could see no sense in jiggery-pokery when it was clearly a choice between right and wrong. McAulay had done wrong. He should be forced to put things right. It was as simple as that to Donald, but his advocate seemed so sure of himself, so comfortable with all this legal intrigue, that he deferred to McLean's superior education and left it in his hands. It was arranged for the farm to be auctioned before Sheriff George Frederick Brown, at Cookshire, on the 18th of September, 1886, at eleven in the morning.

McAulay, as Mr. McLean had happily predicted, objected strenuously to the sale. He had an investment to protect and calculated his expenses in connection with this mortgage at $217 already, but there was nothing he could do. The property, technically, was to be sold in default of debts owed by old Murdo to his youngest son, in payment of a cash loan and nearly two years back wages, and the major had no say in the matter. All he could do was attend the proceedings and make sure the place was not sold for less than the value of his mortgage.

McLean, smilingly, opened the bidding at $200. McAulay quickly jumped it to one thousand. Donald, on a nudge from his lawyer, bid eleven hundred and the farm was knocked down to him. It was over.

When it came time for payment, however, the sheriff asked for an immediate cheque. McLean, on Donald's behalf, formally requested three days of grace in which to arrange details. McAulay saw his chance and objected. He engaged the sheriff in a whispered conference. The sheriff announced that the terms of the sale were strictly cash. Mr. McLean's smile did not waver. McAulay formally offered his cheque for a thousand dollars and the property was made his. Donald was aghast. Mr. McLean rubbed his soft hands and beamed with joy as if a trap were sprung.

"But McAulay's got our farm!" hissed Donald.

"Purely a technicality," smiled Mr. McLean. "I do assure you of that."

"'A technicality?"

"The case comes to trial next month and all will be made clear. Trust in me."

"And where do we live until that happens, then?"

"Stay there, Mr. Morrison. Maintain possession by all means. Possession, as you may have heard, is nine tenths of the law. Trust in me."

Again the advocate smiled with blissful confidence and

again Donald was utterly bewildered. It seemed to his untutored eye that McAulay had once more made off with the pie. The cheque he had handed the sheriff would come right back to satisfy his mortgage — this time with the property clinging to it. His purse, on the end of a string, seemed to attract profits with every cast.

"Trust in me," said a smiling McLean without attempting a layman's explanation of all these ramifications. "When the case comes to court next month, all will come clear. I do assure you of that."

But the case did not come to court the next month, nor the next, nor the month after. Instead of pressing the suit, McLean sent Donald a bill for $200 that he could not pay and gave the opposition time to prepare an offensive. On McAulay's behalf, the firm of Yves, Brown and French, filed a brief of possession on the 8th of January. It reached the Superior Court of Sherbrooke on the thirty-first of that month when McLean, for want of his two hundred dollars, refused to plead. Delay was granted. McAulay's lawyers pressed for judgement. McLean still refused to plead and on the ninth of March judgement was granted in favour of Major Malcolm B. McAulay. Donald and his family were given three days to vacate.

Murdo Morrison

Murdo Morrison was a tough old devil. He had been born and raised on Lewis and Lewis men, they say, go in hard and keep on going. Murdo had been going in hard for more than seventy years and fully intended to keep on going for as long as he was spared — summer or winter, in debt or out, fair or foul weather, farm or no farm. Major McAulay and the Courts of Law might slow him down but they couldn't stop him. A Lewis man, they say, can't be stopped. He can't be hanged, shot or drowned and doesn't starve worth a damn.

Lewis is not an hospitable land. It is low and wet, cold and windy with a black bog over most of it. Its rocks are geologically different from everything else in Western Europe and closest akin to those of the Laurentian Shield, to which the island might well have belonged before the continents migrated. It was natural, therefore, with a people so deeply rooted in the soil, that when it came time for "The Flitting," they should turn eyes to Canada.

"The Flitting" had many causes. The Industrial Revolution localized factories in the Midlands where there was water power in plenty and took work from the cottage spinners and weavers. Industry demanded markets and the British Empire opened offices throughout the world. More markets demanded more production, more production meant more sheep, more sheep wanted more pasturage and more and more crofters were pried from their fields and homes to make room for the beasties.

The Napoleonic Wars, securing these global markets for the English Industrialists and their infernal sheep, left a hard depression in their wake. Returning soldiers contributed to the large-scale unemployment and, on the Western Isles, even the curing of the herring was going scant. More and more Scots left every year, more and more cots stood empty until it was said a man might walk the breadth of Lewis and see only empty homes with the doors standing open and the wind whistling through — nothing under the thatch at all but the cold winds of the sea.

It came their time. Murdo and Sophie Morrison packed what they could and took ship for the New World as had so many before and as would so many after. The farms, they heard, were free for the clearing. The woods were running with game, the rivers dancing with fish, sugar ran out of the maple trees and there was neither laird nor landlord anywhere.

They went in hard and kept on going: south from

Three Rivers to Sherbrooke and then east into the high wastelands which the French and British settlers had long considered unfit for human habitation. That made them just grand for Scotsmen. Up in the hills, the climate was harsh and the settlements sparse but men had a chance to live like Highlanders — free and tough and proud.

Murdo and his wife stopped first at Gould, which had been settled by eight Lewis families in 1838 and was now a thriving outpost. Murdo made a farm there and raised both sons and daughters. He went in hard and kept on going. After Donald, his youngest, came along, Murdo put thought to a larger farm and looked toward the government lands still to be had yet further to the east, yet higher in the hills. Four of his neighbours had gone that way in 1852, walking three days through virgin forest until they met the shores of Lake Megantic. They returned with word that the land was good and the big lake full of fish. Murdo packed up and went east, too, pioneered a place in the wilderness and poured his sweat and blood into the land. He had seen his sons and daughters married one by one and had set them up, one by one, on places of their own. The farm he saved for Donald.

But others, too, looked east. John Henry Pope wanted to link Montreal to the sea through the Eastern Townships and the State of Maine. Since it was the age of railroads and Pope was another man who went in hard and kept on going, he had done it. He drove his railroad from Sherbrooke and Eaton through the Scottish settlements to the Lake itself and kept on going. Megantic boomed with the railroad's coming. People began arriving down that iron trail with products, ideas and complications. People began leaving, too. Many young men went west as Donald and Norman McAulay had done to make a bit of money and do a bit of adventuring. Unlike Donald, many did not come home again.

Times they were a-changing. The Government of Quebec was persuading French Canadians to return from textile towns in Maine, Vermont and New Hampshire to settle in the townships the Scots had built. More French Canadians were pressing up the Chaudière River. Progress invaded the Scottish sanctuaries and gave Murdo the disturbing feeling that he no longer had a tight rein on circumstance. He had often caught himself of late — and particularly since the trouble over the mortgage began — thinking of Fate. And if that wasn't senility, it was senility's younger brother.

But he was not worried for himself, nor even for Sophie — although that good woman deserved a bit of rest — for they had known hard times before and still managed a good run. They knew when to hang on with tooth and toenail, when to kick and bite and holler, when to bend with the breeze. They were not made like poplar trees to snap under every contrary wind, for they had never expected much from life from the very beginning, and if the Good Lord wanted them to start all over again from scratch, then scratch they would. They were quite at home with scratch.

Donald, however, was a horse of another colour. He had his father's stubbornness and hardihood, all right, but he had also learned to hope. He knew something of the changing times, welcomed them and expected a great deal. He had helped to build the village of Megantic — he and Malcolm Matheson had cut down the first trees to erect the first building on the site of the village, had rafted lumber and supplies the length of the lake before roads were grubbed out, had seen the rutted track and the few rough buildings mushroom with the railroad's arrival into a respectable village with mills, emporiums, hotels, houses and even wooden sidewalks. He had learned to hope, and Murdo feared that a fatal flaw.

Another flaw which Major McAulay more clearly recognized was Donald's old-fashioned sense of justice, which made him still believe in right and wrong. McAulay had taken his farm and McLean had taken his money. He

couldn't let that rest but he had first to find a place for his
father and mother to live out of the line of fire. Practically
penniless but determined to leave no stone unturned,
Donald went once more to see McAulay.

"Listen," he said, keeping everything strictly business
this time, "between you and me and the cat, we are knowing the right and wrong of this matter. There are two
choices, now. Either I can chase this thing through the
courts — and sooner or later you'll lose or go bankrupt on
legal fees — or we can settle it here and now, man to man."

McAulay had a bad cold in his head and was in no
mood for calculations but he was in no way ill enough to
miss a possible bargain.

"I'm listening," he growled.

"I have to be looking out for the old folks, now," said
Donald. "You owe me nine hundred dollars but I'm willing to give up all claim to the property for eight hundred
cash."

McAulay sniffed sourly and stared at his ledgers. Red ink
always wanted to make him sneeze for some reason even
when he had no cold. Must be the stuff they made it out
of — it was certainly thick and bright enough. Donald was
owed $900 from the property by decision of the courts —
the debt that had forced the sheriff's sale, and one quite as
legal as the mortgage — but affairs had been so muddled
by the machinations of lawyers that McAulay thought he
had an even chance of avoiding it altogether. He had not
got where he was without playing the odds.

He, too, had been a poor immigrant from Scotland but,
after two years in the Union Army during the American
Civil War, he had clawed his way out of subsistence farming to the world of business. Several contracts on the Quebec Central and the St. Francis and International Railway
had made him fairly well-to-do but he had worked hard
for every penny and had made nothing by handing out
cash to all who asked for it. If Donald had the energy and
the resources to pursue his claim through the courts, he

would probably win in the end. Meantime, a lot could happen and the game was worth the candle.

"I'll make you a counter-offer," he said at last. "My expenses in this matter stand about $1750. I'll sell you the farm for that. I'll even carry a mortgage on half."

Donald glared. He rose up and strode to the side of the desk. He stared down at the major's red neck. His jaw was hard and his voice was low.

"You're a liar," he said. "Your figures are lies! You've put no more than a third of that amount in the place in hard cash and you know it."

McAulay wiped his large red nose on a large red handkerchief and dipped his pen.

"Take it or leave it," he said.

"That farm is mine."

"Not any more, sir. Not any more."

"You'll not be taking that farm, McAulay," said Donald, near a whisper. "You'll not be taking that farm before you've paid back what you've stolen."

McAulay raised his watery eye and tried a little military thunder.

"Are you threatening me again, sir?"

"*Yes, I'm threatening you!*" Donald shouted at the top of his voice. "I'll blow your fat head off before you're getting that farm!"

McAulay rose to his feet. He was a big man, heavier than Donald, and intended to bring the full weight of his rank, power and dignity into a barrage that would shrivel the upstart in his socks — then spoiled it all with a horrendous sneeze. He wondered miserably if he should be home soaking his feet.

"I'm offering you the place," said Donald, in control of himself once more while the man wiped his nose and his eyes with that great red handkerchief. "If you just give my money back, then your law costs can stand against mine and you get the property free and clear. If you don't, then by God Almighty and all the saints in heaven, you'll never have that place in peace."

"Get out," said McAulay. "Get out before I have you arrested."

Augusta McIver

Grimly, Donald went house-hunting. It was a discouraging business for, while there were farms in plenty to be had, there were none he could afford without diving deep into debt and he refused to do that. He finally settled on a rough log cabin near Marsden, long abandoned by a discouraged pioneer and beginning to fall to ruin. There was a small barn of sawn lumber, the tiny cabin and a few uneven acres — with scarcely room between the stones to make a kitchen garden. He repaired the place as best he could and moved his parents in. It wasn't much but it was the best they could do for the moment.

Donald's brothers and sisters came down to help get the house made fit and snug. Neighbours helped by contributing all they could spare in the way of furniture, tools and cooking utensils, and did their utmost to see the old folks comfortable. Murdo growled and complained at the everlasting fuss and bother of it all and generally got in the way. Sophie, in her lace bonnet, pretended it was an outing, put the kettle on the stove and started a batch of scones. Donald got away as soon as he could and walked up through the woods to see Augusta.

He took his time and it was dark by the time he arrived. A lantern was alight in the stable and he had a peek inside before going up to the house. It was well he did.

Augusta was alone there milking an old brockle-faced cow and humming to herself in tune with the ringing of milk in the bucket. Two cats sat near on the straw, all attention, awaiting milk themselves. Urgently, plaintively, they called Augusta's attention to their need and Donald grinned when she expertly splashed a stream of warm milk on their whiskers without pausing in her work or her tune. He tiptoed in as the two cats delightedly wiped their faces and licked their paws. He stopped just outside the lamp-lit circle and struggled to put words to the tune she was humming. . . . Ah, yes. "Colin's Cattle."

> "Crodh Chailein mo chridhe,
>   Crodh Chailein mo ghaoil,
> Crodh lionadh nan gogan
>   Crodh togail nan laogh."

She had turned quickly as the first sound of his voice and was all smiles, blushes, perturbation.

"You should be ashamed of yourself, Donald Morrison," she scolded, "creeping up on a girl in the dark like that."

"I am that," said he, squatting down with the cats. "I'm ashamed I've not been doing it more often."

That made her hide her face in the flank of the brockle-faced cow and the milk hiss fiercely in its own white froth. Her brown eyes looked round in a moment more and her face was concerned.

"I heard you lost the farm," she said, "and I'm sorry for it, Donald. Truly I am."

"It's not lost yet. Not yet," he said. "But that's not what I came to see you about." He picked up a straw and chewed on the end of it. "Are you remembering I said I had something important to be asking you?"

There he goes again! She licked her lips, took a swipe at her hair and sent milk so determinedly into the pail that the old cow looked round to see what was all the bother.

"Yes," she said. She meant it to sound off-hand but it came out rather breathless and shrill. "Yes," she said again.

"Well, I was wanting to ask you . . ."

. . . and she once more in her filthy old clothes, looking a sight and smelling of the barn with her hair every which-way and a pair of her father's old wellingtons on her feet and this was the most aggravating man that ever . . .

"I was wanting to ask if you'd be waiting a bit longer for that question."

The milk stopped flowing a moment and then started again. She sent a warm stream right in his eye.

He lost his balance and fell over backwards out of the light and came up flailing, grinning, licking milk from his moustache.

"Hey! What was that for then?"

"Don't you come around here any more, Donald Morrison." She said it very evenly and concentrated on finishing her work.

"Now, wait," he said. "I didn't mean . . . It's just . . ."

"And I will thank you not to be spluttering about like that. You are disturbing my cow."

Donald said no more but straightened up and waited with a smile until she finished the milking. When she stood up with her pail in one hand and her stool in the other, he took her firmly by the shoulders.

"Augusta," he said, trying to look her in the eye. "I just wanted to say that it's not over yet. There's more fighting to be done and I can't be asking yet. Not yet. Just wait a bit longer until things are steady."

"I don't know what you are talking about, Mr. Morrison."

"Yes, you do."

She would not look at him. He was certainly the most irritating man she had ever met — always creeping up on a girl when she wasn't prepared and then slipping away like a thief or an Indian without any goodbye and leaving a hole where he'd been. He seemed to think a girl had nothing better to do than to stand here listening to his jabber and feeling his cool blue eyes upon her. She felt

his hands still firmly holding her shoulders, felt him waiting silently and patiently for his answer. She chewed her
lip. She raised the stool between them and rubbed her
nose with a finger. She nodded.

"Thank you," said Donald.

Her father bellowed from the yard and Donald turned,
slipped out into the dark and was away.

Donald Morrison

Possession was nine-tenths of the law and Donald would
maintain possession of his property come what may. With
his parents safely installed in Marsden, he could squat on
his farm until the crows came home to roost. He could
turn it into a fortress if he wished with a barricade at
every door and a gun at every window and then just let
McAulay and his help try to throw him off.

But the major's strategy avoided pitched battles. When
Donald returned to the farm on the hilltop, he found the
man had already been at work turning a profit. Four telegraph poles lay at the edge of the woods — tall, straight,
freshly cut and freshly peeled. They would bring a good
price from the railroad and the major had his purse on the
end of a string once more — himself the contractor paying
himself the supplier.

Trouble was, they were not McAulay's poles nor yet the
railroad's poles. They were Morrison poles cut from Morrison trees in Morrison woods and Donald wasn't about to
let the major steal again. He went to the house for his saw
and bucked each pole into firewood.

"There," he said to himself when the work was all done
and the perspiration was running off him. "Let's see the
red-faced old bugger get any satisfaction from that lot."

When the men who had cut and trimmed and peeled
the poles for McAulay came back with a waggon to pick

them up, they discovered the crime and reported straight-way to the major. The major had no doubt of the culprit and reported straightway to the police. The police knew their duty and Constable Edwards was sent straightway to bring Donald in.

William Edwards didn't care much for his mission. He was a long-time neighbour of the Morrisons and had known Donald nearly all his life. He also knew Major McAulay and if he won *that* gentleman in a raffle, he said, he'd swear off gambling for life.

"But I have to take you in just the same, Donald," he said. "It's my duty and all."

"That's all right, Bill," said Donald with a smile. "Just let me lock up here and I'll go quietly."

Driving along together towards town, Edwards asked if Donald had cut up the major's telegraph poles.

"I did," said Donald.

Don't blame you," said the officer. "McAulay's been at his games for years and it's high time somebody stood up to the man."

He went on to narrate several examples of others in the community who had suffered at McAulay's hands and wished Donald great good luck in his court fight.

"He's a scheming, miserly, black-hearted old dragon," said Donald, "and I'll have justice out of his hide sooner or later, one way or another."

But again McAulay triumphed. Donald wound up with the choice of paying fifty dollars or going to jail. It burned him mightily to submit but if he were locked up, the major would be free to do what he wanted with the farm and he couldn't allow that. He paid and hurried home.

McAulay, however, had again wasted no time. When Donald got back to the hilltop farm, he found the door broken in and all his worldly goods thrown out into the weather.

There was little doubt in his mind just who had ordered this outrage but suspicion was not proof. He played the

legal game and began cautious enquiries among his neighbours, proceeded with care and eventually unearthed two
men and a boy who admitted the act on instructions from
the major. It was now Donald's turn to swear out a com-
plaint. He had McAulay dead to rights at last and pre-
ferred charges of forcible entry against him.

The first time the case came to court, the hirelings
failed to appear to testify as they had promised and the
case was postponed. Donald appealed to them. They gave
their word once more but failed to appear a second time
and again the case was postponed. When the witnesses
didn't show up for the third time, the case was thrown out
and McAulay was safe.

He seemed able to do just what he liked with the
machinery of the law, and this rankled in Donald more
than anything else. Justice may be blindfolded but the
man with money and influence was nearly always sniffed
out in the end. While Donald's appeal on the legality of
the mortgage was still in the courts, while his $900 judge-
ment was far from settled, Major McAulay openly put the
property up for sale. He would have liked nothing better
than to muddle affairs still more, to clear his books of the
matter and get out with a modest profit but he could find
no buyers. Almost every Scotsman in the country had heard
of the troubles and one and all sympathized with Donald.
They would not have taken the farm wrapped in red rib-
bons and bows and Donald maintained possession, sat
tight, and awaited the decision of the Court of Review.

Eventually, McAulay obtained a legal eviction order
and Donald was put off by the sheriff. He went quietly,
for he had no quarrel with the police as yet, sneaked back
and took possession once more. The major would have to
go through the whole business again and again to keep
him out at a great deal of trouble and expense and Donald
was hoping to force him into breaking the law by sending
hired men once more. The major, however, refused the
bait, held his temper, and bided his time.

But Donald could not squat forever. He needed to earn a living, needed money to pay the continuing legal fees, needed occasional journeys to Sherbrooke and Montreal for consultations with lawyers. Major McAulay realized this and bided his opportunity. When Donald returned from one such trip, he found strangers living in his house.

On July 1st, 1887, M. Auguste Duquette, knowing nothing at all of the troubles, had showed up in McAulay's office and offered fifteen hundred dollars for the place. The major did not think it necessary to burden the poor man with all the legal history — in fact he had enough trouble keeping his delight from showing — and the bid, after minimal haggling, was accepted. New deeds were made out. Duquette and his wife moved innocently on to their new farm.

It was Donald, then, who apprised them of the situation. He maintained the farm was his and not McAulay's to sell and advised them to leave as soon as possible.

Duquette, quite naturally, went storming back to the major. He had been misled and wanted no trouble and unless McAulay could prove he had clear and legal title to the land, he wanted his money back. McAulay could prove legal title, of course — could prove clear ownership to all but the most diligent of lawyers. The Superior Court at Sherbrooke had tested his original mortgage and found it binding. He had purchased the place outright at a sheriff's sale and cleared the debts. It was his quite plainly and Donald Morrison was just as plainly a madman and a ruffian. He offered to have the man arrested if Duquette cared to bring charges. Ordering them off the farm could be interpreted as a threat — particularly when the man's past history of threats and violence were taken into account. Why, the villain had threatened physical violence to the major on two separate occasions and it was only out of consideration for the boy's aged parents that he had not had him jailed himself.

Duquette was mollified. He had no interest in bringing

charges and Donald had, after all, been quite polite in informing him of the troubles. You wouldn't know to look at him that the fellow was such a maniac but if he made any trouble again, then he would see about having him arrested. Meanwhile, he would farm the land he had sunk his savings into.

Mme Auguste Duquette

The warmth of an oil lamp shone from the kitchen of the house on the hilltop and set the raindrops flashing. Donald saw it as he stood on the road with a sack of oatmeal on his shoulder. He was cold, wet, tired and discouraged and had a long walk yet ahead of him. It wasn't right. It just wasn't right at all. These strangers had no business sitting warm and comfortable and dry in his house while he stood like a beggar outside in the rain.

Without thinking about it, without any thought in his head but to have a look at these usurpers and see how they were treating his home, Donald dropped his sack in its bit of canvas in a sheltered spot against the barn and crept up through the rain to the window. Duquette and his wife were getting ready for bed. Duquette had his stockinged feet on the stove and was yawning and scratching his belly through his shirt. The woman was talking to him in French and doing something with a clock on the shelf — winding it probably. She looked like a potato. They both looked like potatoes. They just had no right to be so comfortable in his home.

Donald pulled his revolver from his pocket and carefully put a bullet past the woman's ear into the face of the clock.

He heard the woman squawk while he was ducking along the wall of the barn to his sack, heard the man shout as he vaulted the fence and stepped into the woods. He

turned beneath the dripping trees and looked back towards the house in time to see Duquette stick his nose out
the door with a rifle in his hand. The light behind him
made the man an excellent target while leaving him unable to see a thing in the dark. Donald cheerfully fired his
finger at him—poof!—and walked through a corner of their
woods back towards the road.

They'll be spending a poor sleepless time in that house
this night, he thought to himself. They'll be listening for
ghoulies and ghosties and lying a-quake all night waiting
to be murdered in their beds. They had a hole in their
window to remember him by and a new keyhole in their
clock and it served them right for taking another man's
house away.

The rain seemed to be slowing a little and it might even
clear off to give him a bit of a moon to light his path. He
could do with a bit of moon for company. He tried a little
whistling but it didn't sound right and he soon gave up.
He didn't really feel like whistling. Doubts were gnawing
away at the back of his mind, nibbling secretly and surely
away at his satisfaction like mice at the baseboard. He
drove them off time and again but they always came creeping back to nibble some more until his comfort was in
shreds and he was forced to face them. Why should
Madame Duquette be punished for something Major
McAulay had done? Hadn't poor Auguste bought the
place in all innocence and honesty? Why should a decent
man like himself be skulking about in the rainy dark and
frightening good citizens half to death? It was a poor thing
to have done, now that the mice were in the light — a petty
thing, like a small boy kicking the cat because he was
afraid to put a boot to his big brother.

Ach, but there was no sense in moaning over it. It was
done and that was that. He wasn't afraid of Major
McAulay and he might just give him an extra boot when
it came time for the kicking for driving him to small
revenges. Ach, there was no sense moaning.

Malcolm Matheson

Malcolm Matheson owned and operated a general store in Megantic that offered plow-points, nightshirts, seed and feed, oranges, canned goods, snuff, gum-boots, stationery, harness buckles, bottled sweets and almost everything else. There was sawdust on the floor, barrels here and barrels there, a big brass spittoon and a great round iron stove surrounded by broken chairs, upturned crates, a checkerboard all ready and waiting.

He was thirty-nine and Lewis-born — blue-eyed, fully-bearded, crowned with an unruly shock of hair — and he was also pensive, slow, stubborn as an ox once the facts were all in and his mind made up. He had pioneered Megantic, built his store in the wilderness and watched the town grow up around it. He had known Donald all his life. Donald had helped him clear the trees and build his store and worked for him for some time before he went for a cowboy. Malcolm knew nothing but good of him.

His store, receiving visits from most of the local people and entertaining many of the older, more philosophic folk about the iron stove, was a clearing house for news and gossip. When word came in, a few days later, that Donald's arrest was imminent, Malcolm found reason to hitch his horse to his buggy and make a special trip to Marsden.

He found Donald with his father, bucking cedar poles and splitting them down for fence-rails.

"Morning, Murdo. Donald."

"Good day, Malcolm. How's you then?"

"Fair to piddling. Yourselves?"

Malcolm sat on the seat of his buggy with the reins beneath his thigh and carefully stuffed his pipe.

"And what brings you out here this fine day?"

"Well, now," said Malcolm, slowly, frowning over his tobacco and feeling his words like so much shoddy goods and having as little trust in them. "Well," he said, "seems someone fired a shot through a window a few nights back and busted a good clock, so they did."

He did not look at Donald but gave all his attention over to his pipe. Donald did not look at his father but could feel the old man's eyes upon him just the same. There was no way out. He tugged at his moustache uncomfortably.

"That was me," he said.

"Seems," said Malcolm again without surprise and taking the devil's own time finding his matches, "that McAulay's sworn out a warrant for your arrest."

Donald's father spat loudly, once on each palm, and went disgustedly back to work. If the damn fool was in trouble with the police, he had only himself to blame. An honest man stays clear.

"For assault?" asked Donald.

"Arson."

"How's that?"

"You heard aright."

"Arson?"

"Seems," said Malcolm, "the house and barn burned down last night."

Donald stared and his father ceased his work behind. Assault was one thing and often excusable in the rough and tumble of pioneer life but arson was something else entirely. Fire was greatly feared in all the wooden houses and an incendiary was thought the most cowardly fiend in all creation. Malcolm risked a glance at Donald's face. There was no mistaking his genuine shock and surpise.

"Burned?"

"Seems like."

"Anyone hurt?"

"Not yet," said Malcolm, watching Donald closely. Donald caught his meaning, nodded twice and tugged at his moustache in anguish.

"Yes," he said, "They *would* think it was me that did it."

"Aye," said Malcolm flatly.

Donald reached up and pulled a pinch of balsam needles from a fir on the fence-line and put them in his mouth. Malcolm puffed on his pipe and looked across the trees to the Megantic Mountain. His horse cropped gently at the grass and old Murdo went back to work. He had no time for all this tom-foolery.

"All right," said Donald, feeling the sap of the balsam like acid on his tongue. "I was in Spring Hill last night but they won't be taking my word for it. I'm sure of that. I've had some experience with the Courts of Law, so I have, and they'd just as soon throw me in jail as not. That will give McAulay just what he wants. I'll not be doing that."

"You'll be hiding then," said Malcolm and it wasn't a question.

"Just for a bit," said Donald, picking up his coat. "Just until this blows over."

"Aye," said Malcolm. "I've a bit of a cabin down by the lake you can stay at, if you've a mind."

Donald nodded and suddenly grinned. He realized that Malcolm had all this thought out before he had come and had simply been waiting for Donald to arrive at the same conclusions. He knew Donald would not have set fire to a house and barn and also knew he would not be eager once again to throw himself on the justice of the courts.

Donald climbed up onto the buggy. He looked back down at his father, at the fence unfinished, the field untilled, at the cabin in need of a new roof and the barn wanting straightening. His father worked on in grim silence, looking suddenly old and very frail.

"'Soiridh,'" said Donald softly.

The old man nodded up. "Soiridh." And went fiercely on with his work.

McAulay, bitterly recalling the threats made in his office, the destruction of his telephone poles, the trouble over the eviction, the disturbing of Duquette and, above all, the expenses incurred in the continuing court fight, was certain that Donald was also guilty of shooting through the window. He had tried to pressure Joe Morin, the Justice of the Peace, into making out a warrant against him for "assault with intent to kill or maim" but there was no evidence to support such a serious charge and Morin had flatly refused.

The firing of a house and barn was a different matter. McAulay marched straight back to Morin and insisted that, this time, he do his duty. Morin protested that there was still no evidence against Donald. McAulay reminded him of the threats, of the destruction of property, of the continual resistance of legal eviction orders, of his harassment of Monsieur Duquette, of his reputation as a gun-carrying trouble-maker and demanded what further proof was needed and whether the Justice of the Peace would wait until someone was murdered before taking action.

Morin, reluctantly made out the warrant. It was given to Constable Edwards to serve.

Edwards took the trip to Marsden with the warrant in his pocket and the weight of his duty on his shoulders. He, also, could not believe Donald guilty of arson. He had inspected the ashes and could find no reason to suppose the fire had any but natural causes. In Marsden, he was vastly relieved to find his bird had flown.

He sat down to have a cup of tea and a little chat with Murdo and Sophie. He didn't ask questions outright but relied upon them to tell him what he had to know and he was not disappointed. Murdo said that his son had admitted firing the bullet that had damaged the clock and called him a damned young fool for it. He would have told the boy that to his face, too, except that the lad seemed quite aware of it already. He also informed Bill Edwards that Donald had denied any knowledge of the fire and, although his son might occasionally be a rash young fool, he was certainly no liar. Besides, he claimed he was with Murdock, his brother, at Spring Hill on the night of May 30th when the fire broke out. Edwards nodded and changed the subject. It was a simple matter to check. If it was up to him, he wouldn't even bother verifying the alibi for he had never found cause to doubt the word of any Morrison. He well understood the pioneer dependency on friends and neighbours where a man's reputation was quite literally the full extent of his fortunes. He also knew that Murdo, a fierce Presbyterian all his days, would not tell a lie even to save his son and that was that. Donald was innocent of arson.

But the wheels of law are impersonal, relentless, amoral and are moved by momentum more than justice. McAulay continued to prod Morin to have that warrant served and Donald put where he could do no more harm. Edwards was instructed to keep his eyes and ears open. He did. Once or twice, the constable's eyes were open wide enough to actually see Donald on the street of Megantic and he was forced to look quickly elsewhere. Again, he received a report that the fugitive had just been seen heading north on the railroad track but, by the time he had questioned his informant closely to be sure there was no mistake as to the man's identity, borrowed a buggy and had his horse reshod, whoever it was had already disappeared. Sometimes the constable bumped into things.

Donald understood the extent of Edwards' dilemma and did his level best to avoid causing embarrassment by staying out of sight as much as possible. If a man had to walk about all day staring at the sky, Malcolm pointed out, he ran grave risk of tripping over his feet and doing himself an injury.

But McAulay was immune to sympathy. He had known for years that treachery lurked all around him, that people only waited for your back to be turned to steal you blind, that Donald had friends and accomplices everywhere and, when he saw the villain walk calmly past his office one morning in broad daylight, he went storming back to Morin and demanded action. It was his civic duty to obtain protection for honest citizens, he thundered. This culprit was known to carry twin revolvers about in his pockets and to be a dead shot with either hand. He had threatened an officer and a gentleman on his own premises. He had threatened Duquette and narrowly missed murdering his wife. He had set fire to a house and a barn and then avoided arrest. How could life and property ever be safe with such a dangerous lunatic loose in society? It was criminal the way a duly appointed officer of the law not only failed in his duty but openly connived, sir, to thwart the law, sir! In the army, a man would be summarily shot for such dereliction.

Morin patiently heard him through and wearily shook his head.

"I am sorry, major," he answered. "But I've done about all the law allows."

"Then why isn't Morrison behind bars, sir? Behind bars where he belongs?"

"Well," said Morin, spreading his palms, "it appears that no one but you thinks the man set those fires. Bill Edwards certainly doesn't."

"Then get someone else to serve that warrant, sir."

"Who? Everyone feels the same way."

"All right," said McAulay, playing his ace. "Then if I bring you a man unafraid to do his duty, will you swear him in as a special constable?"

Morin considered. He was suspicious.

"That depends on who it is."

"Jack Warren, sir. His name is Jack Warren."

"Warren? I can't deputize him. A special constable must

be a man of good character and Warren is a known whiskey smuggler."

"Can you prove that, sir?"

"It's public knowledge. He'll tell you so himself. Heaven knows he's bragged of it often enough to others."

"I want him deputized, sir."

"And I tell you, Major, I can't do it."

McAulay considered as he moved about the room and then came near and lifted a buttock to the corner of Morin's desk. "Listen, Joe," he said, waxing confidential, "you owe me a favour or two I think." He paused. Morin tried to remember where he had incurred the debt. "But if you won't do this for friendship, then I'll make such a bother in the district that you won't sleep nights." He raised a finger as he lowered his voice. "I'll see you answer a lot of unpleasant questions. I'll see Edwards is bounced off the force for dereliction of duty."

"Edwards is a good officer."

"I can bring criminal charges if I have to, sir. I can make things very tough all around and you know it. I want Morrison put away, sir, and if you won't do it, then heads are going to roll. Heads are going to roll, sir! Do you hear me?"

Morin's first reaction was to resist this moral blackmail. His second was to calculate the amount of weight McAulay had to throw around and he had to admit the major had considerable political brawn and could make things very difficult if he was so inclined. His third reaction was to seek a compromise.

"All right. I'll see what I can do but there must be someone else besides Jack Warren."

"Name him."

Morin couldn't and the major would not be brushed off. He did not leave the J.P.'s office until he had a firm appointment for the swearing-in of Jack Warren.

Jack Warren

Lucius Warren — known as Jack to all his cronies — was a large and burly American who had lived in and about Megantic for four years. He boarded at the American House and was known to take frequent "hunting and fishing trips" along the border. Little doubt was left in the mind of anyone willing to stand him a drink as to the true nature of these journeys. Jack fancied himself a hard-drinking, hard-living adventurer and general desperado right out of the dime novels and hinted more than once at being north of the line because things were too hot for him back home.

He didn't know Morrison but he had heard of him from talk in the barrooms. He had heard of Donald's reputation as a good man with a gun and often proclaimed himself a better. He had heard of the reluctance of Constable Edwards to make an arrest and proclaimed it to be cowardice in the face of Donald's reputation. He announced that if he ever met the man there would be no hesitation.

McAulay had heard and McAulay had understood. This was the man for the job.

And this was the man who presented himself at the office of the Justice of the Peace, St. Francis District, to be sworn in as special constable for the sole purpose of arresting Donald Morrison.

Morin was in a foul mood. He looked Warren up and down with obvious distaste and growled at his clerk.

"Where's that oath, then?"

The clerk smiled to himself, reflecting cheerfully on the utter helplessness of all justices and the superiority of all clerks. He knew it was merely the property requirement that stood in the way of a certain superior clerk from becoming Joseph Napoleon Thibaudeau, J.P.

"Section second," he murmured from behind his inky fingers, "Chapter first, Title seventh."

"Yes. Yes. I've got it," grumbled Morin as he found the place in his book. "Raise your right hand."

"Him or me?" asked Warren. The clerk snickered. Morin glared. Warren grinned and raised his hand.

"Repeat after me. I, Lucius Warren . . ."

"I, Lucius Warren."

". . . Do swear that I will well and truly serve our Sovereign Lady the Queen . . ." (Warren echoed his words, grinning the while.) ". . . in the office of Special Constable for the District of St. Francis without favour or affection, malice or ill will . . ." (Morin winced at the echo of that.) ". . . and that I will, to the best of my power, cause the peace to be kept and preserved . . ." (Morin winced again.) ". . . and prevent all offences against the person and properties of Her Majesty's subjects . . ." (Morin's voice faltered but a sound from his clerk drove him on.) ". . . and that while I continue to hold said office . . ." (Joseph Napoleon Thibaudeau was enjoying his discomfort mightily.) ". . . I will to the best of my skill and knowledge discharge all the duties thereof faithfully according to the law. So help me God." (The J.P. finished in a rush which left Warren far behind and lost. Morin repeated the last few words a second time and reached for the warrant.)

"That's all," said Morin. "Here's the warrant. The pay is a dollar a day."

"Do I get to carry a gun?"

Morin moaned audibly. His clerk snickered from behind his hand. Warren looked from one to the other in confusion.

"As a special constable," said the J.P., unable to look any more at the man, "you are entitled to carry a weapon and we are authorized to issue one to you if necessary. However, in this case, I don't think . . ."

"That's all right. I've got my own," said Warren, proudly, and produced from his back pocket a murderous-looking .48 calibre revolver. "I usually carry it in a holster," he said, waving the weapon about. "Faster that way. She's got interchangeable barrels and can stop a moose if you use her right."

Morin shuddered and looked quickly away from the thing.

"For God's sake be careful with that cannon! And don't use it except in self-defence."

"I know how to handle a Christly gun," Warren retorted in disgust and snatched up the warrant. He turned for the door. Morin breathed a sigh of relief.

"Excuse me, Joe," said the clerk from behind his fingers. "He's not a British subject."

"Haven't you got any work to do?" snapped Morin.

His clerk shrugged and went back to copying papers. Warren had stopped at the door and was waiting. Morin's stomach was beginning to feel uncomfortable.

"So he's not a British subject," he said. "What of it?"

"Shouldn't you administer the oath of allegiance, too?"

Morin thought about that while he stared with hatred at Thibaudeau. "Damned uppity clerk," he thought and then went thumbing helplessly through his book.

"Article 603," murmured the clerk with malicious pleasure.

"I know. I know," snapped Morin and turned grumpily back to the front of the book and began riffling pages until he found it. "Damned pimply faced starveling," he grumbled beneath his breath and Joseph Napoleon heard and smiled beyond his hand once more.

Warren loomed over the desk looking from one to the other with the gun in one hand and the warrant in the other.

"Raise your right hand and repeat after me. I, Lucius . . ."

It was the hand with the revolver.

"*For God's sake,* put that damned thing away!"

Warren grinned. The clerk hung his head and his shoulders trembled as if he were throwing a fit. Morin could feel an ulcer coming.

"I, Lucius Warren . . ."

"I, Lucius Warren . . . but everybody always calls me Jack."

". . . Do swear that I will be faithful . . ."

"Or John," said Warren after his litany. "Some folks call me John."

". . . and bear true allegiance to her Majesty Queen Victoria . . ."

"John and Jack's the same Christly thing."

". . . her heirs and successors, according to law — so help me God!"

"So help me God," said Warren. "And don't you worry none. If I get my eyes on Morrison, he won't get no further."

Morin hid his face in his hands and Warren strode out and back to the barroom of the American House. He joined three men at a zinc-topped table who sat far back in their chairs with their caps on and their great boots firmly planted. The warrant, cast challengingly on the table before them, was good for three good drinks right off and the revolver, laid down beside it later, was good for a couple more.

"So you're really going to do it, Jack?"

"Dead or alive."

"I hear he's pretty smart at the shooting."

"You hear that, do you?"

"I suppose he is, at any rate. I've been out west meself and a man in the west is pretty smart at defending hisself."

"And you think I'm not, do you?"

"Oh, I'm not saying that, Jack. I'm not saying that at all. I was just saying what other folks are saying."

"Folks will be saying different before long."

"I suppose they will, Jack. I just suppose they will."

Number two stirred himself.

"I hear tell they once set potaties on a fencerail, so they did. Morrison galloped by on his horse and shot them off. Shot them all off from the gallop, he did."

"Do potaties shoot back?" growled Warren, fierce under his brows. "Ain't she a different thing entire?"

"I suppose she is, Jack," said number two. "Now that you mention her, I suppose she is different."

"On my Christly soul," said Warren, emptying his glass, "I'll fix him if I get my eye on him."

Number three was a short and stocky man with a full beard and the blue eyes of a Scot. "Good luck to you then," he said as he got to his feet. "You are going to need it."

"Who the hell are you?" growled Warren but the young man did not answer. He walked out of the hotel and down the boardwalk to Malcolm Matheson's store. Malcolm was smoking his pipe and overseeing a checker game between two "Companions of the Iron Stove."

"Good day, John," he said. "Fine weather we're having."

"It is that," said John McLeod, fiddling with his beard. "Is anyone knowing where Donald is this day?"

"Mayhap," said Malcolm.

"I was just in the American House," said John. "Jack Warren's been sworn in and has Donald's arrest warrant with him."

Malcolm puffed in thoughtful silence.

"He's saying he'll kill him if he gets the chance."

Malcolm nodded and puffed and nodded again.

"Or Donald might be killing him," he said.

"He might if he's cornered," said John.

Mac McLean was one of the checker players. He stretched himself and stood up.

"I was losing this damn game anyway," he said.

McLean rode out to Malcolm Matheson's camp and found Donald doing a quiet bit of fishing.

"Catching anything, are you?"

"Dyspepsia is all," said Donald. "I'm getting mortal sick of my own company. What's new in town, then?"

Mac sat himself down in the grass and told all he knew of Warren and his boasts. Donald was mildly surprised.

"Will he shoot me, then, on suspicion of burning a barn?"

"Likely he'll shoot because you're known as a good man with a gun," said Mac, "and he wants to be known as a better."

"That's a fearful load for a man to carry," Donald replied with some bitterness. "I smell the stink of McAulay behind all this."

"He was sworn in all legal."

"McAulay took my farm all legal, too." Donald chewed a grass-blade and stared at the sunlight shimmering on the water. "I guess that's the way of the law these days. Why would they be wanting to swear in a man like that?"

"Will you be shooting back, then?"

Donald considered this quiet question and then shrugged and smiled.

"Ah, now," he said, "a man's got a right to protect himself, has he not?"

"Maybe a duty," said Mac as he gnawed on the knuckle of his thumb and stared across the lake to Moose Hill and Tumbledown Mountain in the State of Maine. He was thinking of Mrs. McLeod's clotheslines.

"I'll tell you one thing," said Donald, "I won't be letting him shoot me down like a dog."

Mac said nothing.

"And I'll tell you another, since you ask," said Donald. "I won't be turning myself in, either. Not just yet, anyway. I did not burn that house or barn but I'm convinced there'll be no justice for me in the courts. I've tried it, Mac. There's no justice for us poor gillie-wetfoots and I'll not stand trial for a crime I did not commit if I can help it."

McLean stood up and stretched. "Aye," he said. "I'd best be heading home. If you're needing a place to stay sometime, come by the house."

Donald reached up his hand.

"Thanks, Mac," he said. "I might just be doing that."

Jack Warren

Donald stayed clear of the roads and clear of the village but generally managed to find out what Warren was up to one way or another. Any move the new constable made, any boast or threat, was duly noted and reported in Matheson's store. There it was considered, discussed, adjudged and relayed on to Donald. He heard that Warren journeyed twice to Marsden with his gun in his holster, made a general nuisance of himself and boasted to all who would listen. He heard that Warren had installed a target behind the American House and occasionally demonstrated his expertise with his pocket cannon. He heard that Warren had swaggered into Matheson's store one Monday morning and asked Malcolm point-blank if he knew the whereabouts of his quarry.

"I do not," Malcolm had replied after due deliberation.

"If I get my eye on him," Warren had said, "I'll have his Christly soul dead or alive."

And he heard that Warren usually kept close to the barroom or the verandah of his hotel where he could draw his dollar a day and conduct his hunt in comfort.

Donald listened and laid low. It wasn't easy, for he was

a sociable man and life in the woods was a lonely one. He would have liked to visit Augusta and say a few words to his parents, but he dared not put them in jeopardy so he stayed where he was and waited. Sooner or later, he thought, Warren would tire of his charade and go back to smuggling whiskey.

When he heard one Friday that Warren had gone once more to Marsden, he took the opportunity to slip into Megantic for a few small supplies. He could get what he needed and be long gone before Warren returned.

But Warren had changed his mind. It was too nice a day to go manhunting round and about the country. He lingered still on the verandah of the American House, enjoying the afternoon sun and the warmth of a few beers in his belly. Nelson Leet, the hotelkeeper, sat with him and together they idly watched the passing parade of horses, buggies, children and dogs.

Donald Morrison came strolling down the sidewalk with a cane in his hand and no cares in the world.

Warren got his feet off the railing and learned forward in his chair.

"Is that Morrison?"

"The very man," said Leet.

Warren eyed Donald's approach on the opposite side-walk, got up and went into the hotel for his gun. He buckled it on, descended the steps and started across the street.

"Donald Morrison!"

Donald halted and turned. The big man was in the middle of the street and coming on with danger in his eyes.

"Stand clear," said Donald.

The man kept coming.

"Don't you worry about it," he said.

"Stand clear!" said Donald again.

Warren came on with his shoulders raised and his great hands held loosely at his sides.

"Don't you worry."

"Stand clear!" Donald said for a third time.

"Don't you worry," said Warren and snatched for his revolver. Donald leapt off the sidewalk and dropped his cane. The great eye of Warren's pistol followed him and Donald drew and fired.

The sound of the shot ripped a hole in the afternoon and Warren was punched over backward by a bullet in the base of his brain.

He lay quite still with his revolver beside him. Blood welled slowly from a hole in his throat and the sun and the street waited while Donald stared down with his own gun hanging limply from his hand.

The hole in the day healed over. Megantic hummed as if to make up for lost time. People came on the run. Donald put his gun away in his pocket, picked up his cane and continued his walk.

News travelled from man to man, spreading out from the body in the dust like rings from a stone in a pond.

At three p.m. on Friday, June 22nd, 1888, Donald Morrison shot and killed Jack Warren.

Part Two

Silas H. Carpenter

Concentric circles rippled out from the body in the dust and lapped against the boots of Authority. An autopsy was ordered and performed. The bullet had torn the carotid artery, said Dr. Millette, and passed through the spine causing instantaneous death. An inquest was held. Half a dozen people had witnessed the shooting and identified Donald Morrison as the assailant. Depositions were taken. A new warrant was immediately drawn up and issued. This time the charge was wilful murder.

Constable Edwards was again sent to bring Donald in. He visited the log cabin in Marsden and was not at all surprised to find Donald not there. He stayed for a bit of a *strupach* and a bit of a chat and then asked a few questions of the neighbours. None had seen Donald. None knew where he might be found. The news of the shooting was everywhere and the opinion of the Scottish people was well-nigh unanimous — it was self-defence, pure and simple, plain as your nose.

The man had been cheated of his farm. He had been persecuted unjustly. He had been victimized by lawyers, swindled by the courts, bullied, blamed and bamboozled until he had done what he plainly had to do and what any other self-respecting man would have done in a similar situation. Once more Constable Edwards returned to Megantic empty-handed.

Donald remained in hiding. He had not thought it advisable to attend the inquest — considering his rather delicate position in the matter — but he did show up for Warren's funeral. He had seen from the woods that there were only three people there, including the minister, and thought it only decent to pay his respects. It was the best he could do for the man. No one prevented him. No one attempted an arrest. He listened to the service with bowed head and then returned to the woods.

Word of this boldness spread and misplaced indignation lent momentum to the cumbersome wheels of law. The authorities reached out for help and a detachment of Quebec Provincial Police was sent from Sherbrooke. They asked many questions, received few answers and remained empty-handed. The authorities reached yet further for help — reached all the way to Montreal.

Silas H. Carpenter, Chief of the Montreal Detective Bureau, arrived with his assistant, James McMahon, and four other burly detectives to take charge of the manhunt, make a quick arrest and put an end to the affair. They had recently won fame and gratitude for capturing a celebrated murderer named McGrath and did not think Morrison would be much of a problem. He was a rank amateur compared with most of their hardened clients.

Headquarters was established at the Prince of Wales Hotel in Megantic and business was begun with habitual efficiency. Carpenter very soon knew Donald's history, the names and addresses of his friends and relatives. He detailed men to locate and interrogate all these people and painstakingly assembled a description of the fugitive.

"DONALD MORRISON. Age; 30. Height; six feet. Weight; 175 lbs. Complexion; fair. Eyes; blue. Hair; sandy. This man is wanted in connexion with the fatal shooting of LUCIUS WARREN in the village of Lake Megantic on the afternoon of June 22nd, 1888. Morrison is known to be armed and considered EXTREMELY DANGEROUS."

This man, known to be armed and considered extremely dangerous, was lying on his back among the wildflowers in a corner of McIver's hayfield. Augusta sat nearby with her face shaded by a large sun-bonnet, her legs beneath her and her skirt spread out.

"I did not want to meet that man," he was saying as he studied the drifting clouds. "If I'd seen him first, I would have turned away but he was too close. He had the biggest pistol I ever saw in my life. A holster to carry it round in, too. He would have shot me in the back if I'd turned, then. I'm sure of it."

"I know," she said. She was pulling the petals from a daisy one by one.

"I wasn't wanting any trouble. I was never wanting any trouble. I was just wanting my farm and a quiet life and a little justice."

"I know," she said once more.

"I thought I had all my adventuring done when I came back from the North-West, so I did."

She had reached the last petal on the daisy and was absorbed in it with her head down and her face hidden by the hat. "Yes," she said with one petal left. "I know."

He rolled onto an elbow and faced her.

"I can't be letting them take me," he said. "Not yet."

"I know," said she.

"But now I'll have to be asking you to wait a bit longer for that question I promised," said Donald. He reached out and gently turned her face towards him by the chin. Her eyes were large and damp. "Just a wee bit longer," he said.

She bit her lower lip and lowered her eyes. "I know," she said. She plucked the last petal and let it flutter to the earth.

Silas H. Carpenter

Carpenter was not at all prepared for the difficulties his investigation encountered.

Firstly, the supposed friends and relatives of the fugitive were no help whatever. An amazing number claimed never to have heard of a man named Donald Morrison. Others, all too eager to be of assistance to the gentlemen from Montreal, knew of a good half-dozen by that name in as many different localities. Still others claimed innocence of any civilized language and when an interpreter was found willing to translate the Gaelic, the detectives had reason to believe he was intentionally leading them astray. They couldn't be bullied, bluffed, brow-beaten or bribed. Carpenter's men blundered from one settlement to the next without a single solid lead and learned to their cost that these Scotch settlers were the stubbornest, most independent, hardest-headed creatures ever to walk God's earth.

Secondly, the area of the search proved to be forty miles long by twenty wide and Donald could have been hiding in any of those eight hundred square miles of woods and hills, lakes or swamps, or in any one of a thousand isolated farmsteads from Megantic Lake to Dudswell East. He knew the area as he knew his own barnyard and had friends all over. Carpenter's men were far more familiar with the streets and alleys of the city and had friends nowhere.

Thirdly, surnames meant next to nothing in this strange corner of the world. Once a man was entered in the church register, he might never have reason to use his last name again until they carved it on his headstone. If the detectives wanted to speak with John McLeod, they'd find a dozen — of John MacDonalds, a small army. The settlers knew each other by Gaelic side-names, but how could a bewildered detective know if he wanted John the Horse,

John the Hammer or John the Goat? What's more, these nicknames were hereditary so that John the Horse might have a son named John the Horse and, when that got too deep, they often went through life with their Christian names alone as did John Hector, John David, John Gwilliam. In naming all male heirs either John, Malcolm or Donald Carpenter felt they either exhibited a wonderful lack of imagination or a remarkably solid conspiracy.

Fourthly, Donald Morrison had a most embarrassing habit of going about in public, of being seen in broad daylight and then effecting narrow escapes. It began when he coolly and openly showed up at Warren's funeral but that was not the end of his daring. He was almost constantly appearing and disappearing beneath their noses. One officer — since assigned elsewhere — actually questioned Donald at a farmhouse and left believing him one of the family. Another knocked at Mrs. Buchanan's door and politely waited while that worthy woman was helping him out through the pantry window. A third learned from Murdock McIver that Donald had gone to Fisher Hill while the villain was actually listening to the lie from behind the open door. To ease poor Murdock's conscience, he did go to Fisher Hill right after — following the tracks of the unwitting detectives.

Now, Carpenter was a reasonable man. He'd had his share of dangers, difficulties, desperate characters, and merely wanted to do his job with a minimum of heroics and a maximum of cool reason. It was reasonable to expect a desperate criminal to act like one, for instance — to run like a deer, hide like a mouse, fight like a wildcat — but not to be walking right up to his hunters and discussing the weather. It was reasonable to expect people to speak English or French in this province and not be coughing and gargling in a tongue left over from the stone-age. It was reasonable to expect John McLeod to answer to his name and not be known by something odd that his grandfather had done.

Carpenter knew he would never win the confidence of these unreasonable people, never understand their alien ways, never quite get used to discussing the weather for five minutes before getting down to any sort of business, never feel at ease accepting tea and scones from a people determined to part with nothing else. He also knew his time was limited. His forces were on temporary loan from other departments and agencies and had been spared only briefly and grudgingly. His superiors kept clamouring for an arrest or, at the very least, for hard information that might justify his expenses. And, to top it all off, his hemorrhoids were acting up.

He took to the roads himself, partly to avoid the telegraph and partly to find some sense in his predicament. He drove aimlessly about day after day, from one settlement to the next, receiving hospitality and silence wherever he stopped. Travelling the narrow roads, he realized that his quarry might well be watching him pass from the heavy cover of the woods on either side. His men were cautious about penetrating those woods and Carpenter could not blame them for that. They seemed created to hide things far more ferocious than criminals and he would have had a hard time explaining to Montreal if his officers got themselves eaten. They had even managed to get lost on the roads until they realized the settlers were taking perverse delight in giving false and confusing directions. Carpenter himself spent one entire morning stuck at a ford on a remote, deserted track and it was only after two men on foot had cheerfully heaved his buggy out and sent him on his way, that he realized the taller man fitted the description of Morrison perfectly. He hurried back to the spot but could find no trace of either man and narrowly missed getting stuck again. Days on the hard buggy seat over rutted roads only exacerbated his delicate condition and, when he finally returned to the Prince of Wales and a sheaf of new telegrams, he admitted the job was too much for him and took the next train to Montreal.

They listened politely enough — listened when he spoke of the scattered settlements and the bad roads and the miles upon miles of trackless forest, listened when he spoke of the people, listened even when his desperate quest for reason led him rambling through Scottish history for examples of fierce independence and a shielding of fugitives that was almost traditional — of Wallace and Bruce, of Bonnie Prince Charlie and Rob Roy MacGregor. They listened and clucked their tongues and then sent him back to Megantic with two more men and authority to offer a three thousand dollar reward.

Donald Morrison

Donald, meanwhile, was getting his visiting done. Wherever he went friends and relatives fed him, sheltered him, gave him the latest news of the detectives and the police. He renewed old acquaintances and made new ones. He discovered new trails through the woods and remembered old ones. He was rapidly learning all the tricks of a hunted fox.

Walking one morning down a lonely road with his stick in his hand and his guns in his pockets, he came suddenly upon two detectives smoking their pipes and sunning themselves on a log. They had seen him and he did not hesitate but walked right up with a smile on his face and wished them both a great good morning.

"And a great good day to you," they said.

"Are you still looking for Donald Morrison, then?" said he, after the usual remarks on the weather.

They pricked up their ears. "We are," said one, a great burly fellow with a square jaw and a trim moustache. "What is it you know of him?"

"I was passing a man about two miles back who was

acting suspicious and all," said Donald. "Mean-looking cuss he was too, with his eyes set close and a scowl on him would scare a cat."

"What was suspicious about him?" asked the second man while the first studied Donald's face with a scowl and suspicions of his own.

"Why, when he saw me coming, he jumped into the brush right off."

Donald stared right back.

"You think that suspicious, do you?"

"It's not the usual way of an honest man," said Donald.

"Come on, McMahon," said the smaller constable, getting up and putting his pipe away. "We'd better check it out." He started down the road.

Donald wished them a cheerful good day and good luck and strode off in the opposite direction. "Always willing to help the authorities," he said.

The big man stayed where he was on the log and stared after Donald with a frown on his face as if trying to remember something. His partner stopped and turned back.

"What's up, Jim?"

"I'm thinking," said McMahon, slow and careful, "that could have been Morrison himself."

The other thought a moment but didn't believe it. Morrison wouldn't walk right up and speak to them, would he?

"Maybe he would," said McMahon.

They looked at each other.

"Maybe," agreed the smaller. "We'd best just check him out."

McMahon drew his Colt and went after the retreating figure.

"Hey!" he bellowed. "Just a minute, you!"

Donald was just rounding a curve in the road and did not stop nor give any indication of having heard. The detectives shouted again and ran heavily after him with their guns at the ready, rounded the bend and found the road empty for a good stretch ahead. Donald had ducked into the trees.

Once free of the road and out of sight, he walked leisurely through the woods for two good miles and emerged on another road that ran parallel to the one he had left. There, he was overtaken by a man in a buckboard and offered a lift. Donald accepted.

"You're Donald Morrison, aren't you?" said the driver.

"I am," said Donald. "And you're John Hall from Dudswell."

"You know me, then?"

"If I didn't, I wouldn't have climbed up here."

"Aye," said John with an appreciative chuckle, "you're the man I've been hearing about all right. If you're ever out to Dudswell, drop in and see us. You'll be safe enough there, I'm thinking. There's not a man, woman or dog would turn you into the police from what I hear."

Donald told him of the narrow escape he had recently had with the detectives and they laughed over it together.

"McMahon was studying me like he'd met me before," he said, "and couldn't quite remember my name. By the time it dawned on him just who I was, I was off and into the bush."

He thanked his new friend once more for the offer of hospitality, jumped down and disappeared into the trees with a wave of his hand. John Hall drove on ruminating on the good story he would tell his friends when he got home until he was stopped by a brace of constables. No. He had met no one. No. He knew of no one answering the description they gave. Could be, the man they wanted might be coming down the other road.

Silas H. Carpenter

Carpenter was getting nowhere at all. He had posters printed naming the amount and conditions of the reward with a description of the fugitive appended and had these liberally distributed in every village and settlement for miles around. There was scarcely a barn or a fence, scarcely a tree or a post that did not shout the name of Donald Morrison but it did no good. It merely made sure no man would harbour a detective by mistake.

He sent men to watch the cabin of Morrison's parents and the house of Augusta McIver. He even spared others, after an unpleasant interview with a blustering Major Mc-Aulay, to guard the residence of that worthy gentleman. He pored over maps of the district, arranged logistics, established outposts and lines of communication and got nowhere at all.

He called for help. He continually called for help. They sent him a detachment of Quebec Provincial Police from Quebec City and a handful of soldier volunteers from a French Canadian Militia Unit.

Out in the settlements, detectives and officers encountered traditional Scottish suspicion while the rank and file received traditional pioneer hospitality. Soldiers and constables, generally farmer's sons themselves, were always willing to discuss crops and weather over a cup of tea or a sly drop of the creature. They had their own resentment of officers and detectives and this intimacy resulted in the sowing of seeds of sympathy among the forces sent to arrest Donald. These seeds were carefully nurtured, meticulously cultivated until they bloomed and cast seeds of their own. Was not Donald Morrison a poor country boy like themselves? Did they not all have experience in one form or another with mortgages and the chicanery of lawyers? Was there any real doubt that Donald had fired in self-defence?

Occasionally, when the soldiers had good reason to believe Donald might be in a particular area, they arranged urgent business to take themselves elsewhere. Occasionally, through staring so hard at the sky, the patrols bumped into things.

"Leave those Frenchmen here another month or two," chuckled Malcolm Matheson to the Companions of the Iron Stove, "and they'll all turn Scotch!"

Malcolm set up lines of communication of his own, often through Mac McLean, the Spring Hill railwayman, or John Morrison, postmaster at Marsden. Donald had possibly the single best mail service in the country and was kept informed as much as possible of the activities of the detectives, of the arrival of reinforcements, of the nature and business of strangers and even, on occasion, of the contents of official letters. He very often knew more about Carpenter's men than did Carpenter himself.

As days and weeks passed without result, Carpenter adopted more desperate tactics. He tried to suborn settlers as he suspected the settlers had suborned some of his men. He threatened, bullied, waved the reward money like a juicy carrot under an ass's nose and found the people as incorruptible as they were stubborn. Three thousand dollars was a small fortune to most of these hard-pressed, hard-working folk but only three were ever known to offer information not calculated to lead the pursuit astray. These three were quickly known to their neighbours and secretly watched to see they could do no further damage.

James McMahon

McMahon led a party of men to a house on the North Hill. Lamps and candles burned in almost every room and the sound of music, of singing and dancing filtered out into the night. It was obviously a party of some sort and the word was out that Donald was a sociable man with a weakness for parties. He might possibly be attending this one but even if he were miles away, it was a good opportunity to impress the citizens with the seriousness of this manhunt and to convince them of the inadvisability of shielding the outlaw.

McMahon sent two men down the road and two more up to block any attempt at escape and led the remaining four to the house. He hammered on the door with his great fist and was gratified to hear the music and laughter stop dead.

The door opened. He barged in without a word. Two men were sent upstairs and two more to search the back while he studied the faces of those about him in the big room. There were five men and three women and none of the faces belonged to Donald. Two attractive young ladies sat on the lounge and giggled behind their hands but he paid no attention. He was on no frivolous business. One young man had the pipes beneath his arm but was too portly to be Donald. An old lady offered him a slice of birthday cake but he ignored her and continued staring from one to the other of the grinning faces about him.

His men clattered downstairs and shook their heads. The others returned from the back and did the same. McMahon went the rounds of the party guests once more as if trying to memorize them all. Each met his scrutiny with a cheerful smile. McMahon led his men outside.

The pipes sent them on their way. A shout of laughter followed. McMahon and his men mounted their waggon and drove off into the night looking for another party to spoil.

Inside the house, Augusta McIver and her sister leapt delightedly from the lounge, reached underneath and dragged a grinning Donald out into the light. The music and dancing continued.

Stories of Donald's bold exploits began appearing in the public press. They were meagre and confusing and left the impression that a two-gun desperado, aided and abetted by the population, was challenging all law and order and terrorizing the district. Rumour, carried from mouth to mouth, had things a little differently. An eager young reporter from the Montreal *Star* decided to dig out the truth.

Peter Spanjaardt was assigned to cover a murder trial in Sherbrooke at the time but the trial proved dull and all the excitement seemed to be coming from the east. He made a few inquiries, cultivated a few contacts and dreamed of entering the lion's den and interviewing this bandit face to face. He journeyed to Megantic and began asking questions.

Malcolm Matheson and his Companions of the Iron Stove understood that Donald could only benefit from having his case fairly publicized but could not be blamed for being suspicious. They had learned something of spies and treachery from Carpenter's efforts to suborn them and Spanjaardt, while a nice enough young fellow, wasn't very Scottish. They made a few inquiries of their own of Spanjaardt's boss, Mr. Hugh Graham, proprietor of the *Star,* a man as Scottish as one could wish and much respected for fairness and honesty.

While Spanjaardt's credentials were thus being checked, he wandered about Megantic talking with the people and learning what he could. He was much impressed by the strangeness of their language, by the firearms in evidence, by the fierce appearance of the men and the white lace bonnets of the old ladies. He learned to ask *"Big mar tha sibh au nuedh?"* in greeting and to answer *"Gart tabi-hibh"* when such was asked of him. He found that everyone had a good word for Donald, the two-gun desperado,

but could unearth none who spoke well of Major Mc-
Aulay. His impressions of the situation began to change
and Morrison began appearing less a villain than a victim.

He visited the farm where all the trouble had begun.
Only one barn remained standing with the burned foun-
dations of the house and the second barn just a few feet
away. The hay was high and still uncut. Rumour had it
that Donald would not allow Duquette to reap his hay
while the detectives were trying to persuade him to do so
immediately in the hope of drawing the fugitive from
cover. Spanjaardt returned to his hotel and filed the first
of many stories on Donald Morrison. He did not neglect
to mention that he had been followed about all day by
two beefy detectives.

A meeting between Spanjaardt and Donald was arranged for the night of August 7th and elaborate precau-
tions taken against pursuit or treachery. Spanjaardt was
instructed to buy a railroad ticket to Sherbrooke and
detectives watched him board the train to be sure he was
really leaving. He got off at the next station, was met
there by a long-bearded man in a buggy and driven north
to Spring Hill. Information was exchanged in the Gaelic
with almost everyone they met along the road and they
did not hurry. They had a meal in Finlay's Hotel and
then drove about until Spanjaardt was entirely lost and
confused and the day was nearly done. They arrived at a
large two-storied house in the middle of a field. A bare-
foot boy, obviously on watch for them, bolted inside with
the news of their coming and Spanjaardt was led, a few
minutes later, into the front parlour. Donald rose from
the corner of a couch and held out his hand.

Spanjaardt was nervous at first, never before having
been closeted alone with a murderer, and Donald felt
awkward about telling his troubles to a complete stranger.
This mutual shyness, mutually recognized, drew them together. Spanjaardt took out his cigar-case. They lit up and
smoked in silence for a few minutes and then Donald

began walking slowly up and down the room telling of his troubles over the mortgage, threaded his way through all the legal jiggery-pokery to narrate the fatal meeting with Jack Warren on the street of Megantic. He did not try to elaborate or excuse but to present the facts as clearly as he was able, trusting the reporter to do his job well in laying his case before the people. By the time he had finished, it was full night, their cigars were reduced to stubs and a bond of friendship had been forged between them that was to last the rest of Donald's life.

They shook hands once more. Spanjaardt was thanked for his cigar and he and his guide invited to stay for supper but they politely declined and went out to their buggy. As they were pulling away, Spanjaardt looked back to see several armed men leaving the house where they had obviously hidden as sentries, fearing treachery after all.

The reporter took the train to Sherbrooke and cornered Major McAulay in the Grand Central Hotel where he had been hiding for several days. He interviewed the major to get both sides of the dispute, to be able to present them fairly, but a question at the end of the interview left little doubt where Spanjaardt's sympathies lay.

"Major," he asked, "are you a real estate dealer, a moneylender or a capitalist?"

And McAulay answered, "I am simply a poor man. When I lend some spare money, I do it just to help people out."

Spanjaardt's story appeared under the circus headlines popular in that period.

"A REBELLION IN MEGANTIC!" they announced. "MORRISON THE MURDERER DEFENDED BY THE YEOMANRY. The Clans In Arms. *The War Correspondent of the "Star" Interviews the Rob Roy of the Region.* An Enterprising Reporter Risks His Freedom and His Life!"

The story fired the imaginations of readers, reporters and editors alike and was the first of many. There is little that people enjoy more than the tale of a poor man successfully defying all the might of Authority, and Donald suddenly found himself with hundreds of new friends and sympathizers. Carpenter suddenly found an increase in the amount and vehemence of his telegraphs and his job that much more difficult. He took the train once more to Montreal.

Murdo McArthur

Two days later, Donald was having a hearty dinner at Murdo McArthur's place near Winslow when the dog barked and the police hammered on the kitchen door. Murdo jumped up and went for his Winchester but Donald stopped him with a shake of his head. He picked up his plate, his knife and fork, and went down into the cellar. He sat on the cellar steps in the dark and calmly finished his meal while the boots of the officers tramped overhead. When they left and all was quiet once more, Donald came up with his empty plate and had a second helping.

Ten miles to the south, Augusta McIver was brushing her hair in front of her glass and humming to herself. She didn't know just what tune it was she hummed until the words came by themselves and made her hands tremble.

"Crodh Chailein mo chridhe,
   Crodh Chailein mo ghaoil,
Crodh lionadh nan gogan
   Crodh togail nan laogh."

And then, without a sound, she dropped her hands to her lap and the tears were running and she just sat watching her face swim in the mirror and feeling the water course down her cheeks like rain on a window, steady and silent, until it ran down her nose and splashed very softly on the washstand. The tears ran down and her shoulders trembled and she sat still and silent, not caring, not even trying to stop, just waiting patiently for it all to come to an end and hearing the words to "Colin's Cattle" go round and round in her head as they were sung by a soft baritone one evening out in the barn.

One hundred miles to the north, Chief Carpenter and James McMahon were attending a very important conference. Honoré Mercier, Premier of the province, had been embarrassed by the continued failure of the police and let it be known quite strongly that he wanted an end to the matter. The whole affair was beginning to look like an insurrection. Attorney-General Turcotte and his deputy, Charles Fitzpatrick, had convened several police chiefs to examine the business. Chief Hughes of Montreal gave it as his opinion that twenty men should surround the district and arrest anyone interfering with the officers. Chief Carpenter, barely concealing his amusement, pointed out that twenty men surrounding eight hundred square miles would leave holes large enough to drive an army through. High Constable Henry Moe, of Sherbrooke, asked where the twenty men could be found and whether the Province would pay all expenses. Chief Carpenter reiterated that twenty men would not be enough. Turcotte asked Hughes if he would take twenty men from Montreal at the Government's expense. Carpenter sighed. Chief Hughes doubted that the city could spare a force of that size and maintained that it was the job of the Quebec Provincial Police. Carpenter wanted to scratch. Turcotte offered Hughes $300 in preliminary expenses with which to examine the feasibility of his plan and restated the Premier's concern in the matter. The meeting adjourned. All but Carpenter and McMahon believed something significant had been discussed and decided.

Carpenter returned to Megantic and things went as

before. Nothing changed but the weather, and that was getting worse each day. Hughes' agents arrived from Montreal, went about for a couple of days with a great show of efficiency and returned to Montreal to report on their thorough investigation. Chief Hughes informed Turcotte that he would need a thousand dollars to take twenty men to surround the district.

Meanwhile, Turcotte was negotiating with a certain merchant of Lake Megantic who suggested Donald might surrender to his friends if the reward money were paid into a fund for his defence. Turcotte demanded a written guarantee from Donald that he would never again molest Major Malcolm B. McAulay. John Leonard and F. X. Lemieux offered to defend Donald in court but then the whole business was leaked to the *Star* and negotiations collapsed. Nothing had changed but the weather.

Malcolm Matheson

Winter gave all the advantage to Donald. He could scurry through the woods on snowshoes with the speed and ease of a rabbit while the police floundered around as helpless as hens. He could travel wherever and whenever he wished while they were often bogged down on impassable roads. He had food and shelter for the asking while their patrols were sometimes snowbound and their outposts abandoned in the face of frostbite. Carpenter adopted a different tactic and sent for Malcolm Matheson.

Turcotte and Mercier had suggested an end to their embarrassment at bargain rates and Carpenter was to establish secret and unofficial contact with the outlaw. Matheson was the logical contact. He was known to be a long-time friend of Donald and his store a clearing house for local news. The comparative ease with which that newspaper reporter had interviewed the fugitive indicated the existence of an underground organization of some kind and Carpenter suspected — although he could not prove — that messages and supplies went rather regularly out from Matheson's store to wherever Donald was hiding. He now wanted to open this channel of communication for a message of his own choice.

Malcolm, however, would be hurried by no man. He sent the detective's messenger back with word that he was busy for the moment but would try to squeeze the Chief into his schedule when he had time. Carpenter put on his hat and crossed the street himself.

"Mr. Matheson," he said. "I should like a word with you in private."

Malcolm was seated by the stove with his feet on a flour barrel, his pipe going full blast, embroiled in a game of cribbage. He studied the detective with one eye closed against the smoke and then took the pipe from his mouth and examined the bowl.

"I'm awful busy," he said at last.

Three other men sat by the stove pretending absorption in their cards but Carpenter would not go away. He stood where he was and waited. He said nothing, did nothing, simply stood still and waited. Malcolm laid down his hand.

"All right," he said, getting heavily to his feet. "Let's be going back to the store room, then."

Chief Carpenter followed him through a rear door to a room piled high with sacks of feed, kegs of nails, boxes and bins, bottles and barrels. They found seats on a couple of sacks and Carpenter got down to business.

"Sometimes," he began, gently, "a policeman's job is a very thankless one. I know we're not popular here for trying to arrest Morrison but we're not popular at headquarters either for failing. They keep clamouring for results. They can't understand why it is taking so much time, money and manpower to bring him in."

Malcolm had his pipe going again and sat with his hands on his thighs and his elbows wide squinting at the detective through the fumes.

"I have a wife and kids, Malcolm. I'd like to be home with them right now. Trouble is, as long as Morrison remains in this area, I have to keep right after him. We can't very well go home and ignore a man who keeps popping up under our feet and making fools of us. We have to keep trying until we catch him no matter how long it takes, no matter how many men we have to use. We'll get him sooner or later, too. You know that."

Malcolm took the pipe from his mouth. "You weren't just wanting to tell me your problems, were you?"

"On the other hand," said Carpenter, still gently and pointedly ignoring the remark, "if Morrison left the district he'd be somebody else's problem. I and my men could go home."

Malcolm eyed the Chief thoughtfully for a long moment. He was beginning to get the drift of the man's talk. Carpenter sat still and waited.

"Would they not be hunting him just as hard wherever he went?"

Carpenter scratched his chin.

"Well, Mr. Matheson," he said, "just between you, me and the tom cat, I sincerely doubt it. I don't think they'd be eager to mount such an expensive search again. It's a matter of economics, do you see?"

Malcolm nodded. He understood. It's a matter of political expediency, he thought, but he didn't say that. "It's a matter," he said, slowly, "of saving face all around."

Carpenter stood up.

"Well," he said, "it's going to be a nice day, seems like."

"That all you wanted to tell me, was it?"

"Unless it snows again," said Carpenter.

He put on his hat and he left.

The Schoolteacher

Donald, next morning, was escorting a lady down a lonely country road. She was the schoolteacher at Galson and knew nothing of her companion except that he was a friend of Murdo McArthur's and had offered to walk her to the school since it was on his way. She was glad of his company for she had heard hair-raising stories of a murderer loose in the countryside and her pupils were sometimes stopped and questioned and it was getting so bad a girl hardly dared set foot outside her lodgings alone any more for fear she'd be jumped on and murdered and she was very glad Murdo had a friend to accompany her this morning for she'd had a dream last night that the outlaw was in the vicinity and she really appreciated the protection of his broad shoulders and sincerely hoped she wasn't putting him out at all.

She chattered away in time with her high buttoned trotters, glancing frequently up at Donald's fine moustache and easy smile. Donald kept an eye peeled for the police, said no word and let her run on and she stopped only at the door of her schoolhouse to turn and thank him kindly and hope they might meet again some time. Donald removed his hat and hoped so too. She bobbed her head and blushed and retreated to the schoolroom. Safely ensconced at her desk she made a mental note to enquire more about the gentleman next time she spoke with McArthur.

John Hamilton

John Hamilton was the shoemaker at Gould. He was a long-faced, taciturn man who lived alone and was always glad of a bit of company. It was there that Mac McLean caught up with Donald.

"Good day, John. Good day, Donald."

"Nice one," they said.

"Cold as a witch's tit," said he.

"Pull a chair to the stove," they said. "Take your boots off."

"I've news from Malcolm Matheson. It seems Chief Carpenter came to see him the other day and made it plain they'd be letting you go if you've a mind to leave the district."

"There you go," said Hamilton.

"Aye," said Donald but he did not seem to share his friend's enthusiasm. "Why would they be doing that, do you suppose?"

"Politics," said Mac, "and money. They figure they've spent too much on you already. Malcolm says they could have sent you to college for less."

Hamilton laughed but Donald was thoughtful. McLean went on with his news.

"And, you know Green? Him that has the pulp mill at Marsden?"

"The Yankee?"

"That's him. He's got a scheme all worked out to be smuggling you across the line on snowshoes. You'd be safe enough in the States, they reckon."

Donald got up and walked to the window where frost ferns were scaling the panes. He stared out for a long moment.

Mac watched him grimly. He turned to Hamilton.

"What *is* the matter with the man?" he asked. "I thought he'd be jumping at the chance."

"I think," said Hamilton, "that he's grown awful fond of my cooking."

"Your cooking is enough to drive anyone abroad."

They studied Donald's back but could learn nothing from it.

"He's a very stubborn man," said Hamilton.

Donald turned from the window and faced them.

"I can't be doing it," he said.

"Why not, then?"

"If I run away, it'll be like admitting I've done something wrong. They'll all be nicely forgetting about the farm that was stolen, about the old folks they threw out of their home, about Major McAulay's grasping ways. I can't be letting them do that."

"You stay here," said Mac, "and they'll shoot you down or lock you up sooner or later."

"I know it," said Donald. "But I have to stay just the same."

"Is that what I should be telling Matheson, then?"

"Tell him," said Donald, tugging at his moustache, "tell him thanks very much but I can't be leaving without my eight hundred dollars. When McAulay gives back what he stole, when he makes things right, then I'll go away and leave him in peace."

Mac shook his head. "He won't like it," he said.

"But somebody's got to be standing up for what's right, don't you see? I can't just be forgiving and forgetting and running off as if nothing has happened. They'd be no meaning in it all. How about my old dad? How about my old mother, then?"

McLean and Hamilton looked at their boots and thought it over. There was sense to his stubbornness.

"That eight hundred would see them comfortable for a good long time," said Donald. "I've got to stay and fight," he said and it sounded like an apology.

"Okay," said Mac. "I'll see that Matheson gets the word."

Donald slapped his friend on the shoulder. "I'd appreciate it," he said. "And thank Mr. Green for his trouble, will you?"

Norman McAuly

The detectives, as if to add weight to Carpenter's offer, got lucky and arrived to search Gould while Donald still stayed with Hamilton. They were hot on his heels. He avoided them in the cemetery and fled south through the woods to Spring Hill. A couple of days later they pried him out of hiding once more and again he fled, dodged them on the roads, lost them in the woods but was kept constantly moving, continually in danger until he wanted nothing more than a good night's rest and a day or two of peace.

He was asleep in Colin Campbell's camp when the door burst open in the night. He came up from the cot with a pistol in each hand, dropped to his knees and prepared to sell his life dearly but a voice he remembered held his fire.

"Don't shoot, for God's sake! I'm carrying a bottle!"

"Norman?" asked Donald, hardly believing. "Is that Norman McAuly?"

"The one and only," said Norman, "and it's a very nervous man you are, Donald."

"Stand still while I get a lamp lighted, you rascal. I don't want you falling down and busting that jug."

The lamp revealed Norman's wry grin and tousled hair, his broad-brimmed hat and his jug. Donald slapped him on the back, pumped his free hand and opened the jug. They had grown up together, gone westward together and ridden together all over the plains and Donald could think of no man he would rather see at that moment than Norman McAuly.

"But what are you doing in this part of the world?"

"Well," said Norman. "I was hearing of your troubles and thought I'd come make you an offer."

Donald leapt up and went to the window. He was worn and haggard, red-eyed and weary, and his ear identified every unusual sound in the woods outside while his eye flicked from door to window and back again.

"Actually, Malcolm Matheson wired me," said Norman, watching his friend with concern. "He thought I might persuade you to come back to the cowboy's life."

Donald checked the door again. "Aye. Malcolm wants me to run away, so he does."

"You're in poor shape, Donald."

Donald stopped, grinned, passed a hand over his head and sat down on the cot.

"Sometimes I fancy a policeman behind every tree and bush," he said. "And I fancy they're all drawing a bead on my belly. It's no good for the digestion, Norman."

"It's a good drink, you are needing."

"Aye. And one of your silly stories."

Norman passed him the jug of apple-jack and Donald took a good long pull and tried to relax. His hands were trembling slightly.

"Did I ever tell you about my uncle Willie, then? Willie the Crump they called him, although I never did know why. He was a terrible man. A terrible man, was Willie. Shingle-weaver by trade. Used to carry his teeth about in his pocket, so he did, and whenever he was around something that needed eating, he'd take them out, polish them up and put them to work."

Donald laughed and had another drink.

"We stole them on him one day and hid them. Poor Willie thought he'd lost them in the hay, so he did, and he went through three loads of the stuff, straw by straw, cursing a blue streak. When we took pity on the poor old man and gave them back, he was mad enough to chew nails and spit rust. Always wore them on his watch chain after that, like a pearl brooch."

Donald was beginning to relax.

"Was there a point to that story I might have missed, Norman?"

"None that I know of," said Norman. "Pass the bottle."

Donald chuckled. "Ah, you're very good for me, Norman. How's things in the west?"

"Quiet," said Norman. "Awful quiet since they hanged Riel."

"Hanged the rascal, did they?"

"They did that. What's this? Books? You are reading books on the sly and secret, Donald Morrison. Oh, it's a sad thing you've come to. Charles Dickens and the *Tiomnadh-Nuadh*. I never did think to see the day you'd become the fool of books and that's the truth."

"I've given up drinking and dancing for a spell," said Donald with a grin. "Have to do something in the evenings."

"But it's terrible to see a good man going to the bad."

"Did you never read a book yourself, Norman?"

"Aye. I did once, I must confess. Stole it from my sister. Had a lot of kissing in it, as I remember. Kiss, kiss, kiss. Awful, it was. I had to read it out of the edge of my eye, I was that embarrassed."

They talked and joked and teased each other far into the night and Norman kept passing the jug. Donald could feel the strain of the past few days leaving his body and being replaced with warmth and good fellowship and eventually he fell asleep — slept with a smile on his face and more soundly than he had for weeks — while Norman kept the watch.

He was wakened late in the morning to the smell of a hearty breakfast. Norman had eggs and ham and strong coffee all ready and Donald felt like a new man. They talked of bunkhouses and of breaking horses, of trail camps, and roundups and people and towns but Donald could not be budged. He had made up his mind to stay in the district as a terror to McAulay and a thorn in the side of the authorities, to get as much publicity and sympathy for his cause as he was able and see it through to a finish. He would not run.

Norman suggested they borrow horses and go riding together — hoping the squeak of leather and the pounding of hooves might yet do what words could not. They raced each other down the empty roads, shouted and laughed and remembered old times. Donald chattered along with some of his old cheeriness but still kept a wary eye out fore and aft, to left and right.

He was first to spot the buggy cresting a rise ahead of them. He reined in and scrutinized its passengers.

Neither of the two men were detectives or even constables but it was a moment before he could make out just who they were. One was Major Malcolm B. McAulay and the other his bodyguard.

Donald's face split into a wide grin.

"Norman, my lad, are you ready for a bit of fun?" he asked.

"I am," said Norman.

"Then do you see who that is coming towards us?"

"I do," said Norman.

"Then whip up your horse and we'll give them a scare!"

They raced ahead side by side and were upon and right past the buggy in an instant. Donald reined in suddenly as if just recognizing its passenger. The passenger had done some recognizing of his own and dived for the floorboards to make himself as small a target as possible.

"It's McAulay," yelled Donald at the top of his lungs. "After the devil!"

Norman gave an ear-splitting imitation of an Indian war-whoop and the buggy shot off with the bodyguard whipping the horses unmercifully and the major rattling about in the bottom while the cowboys sat their mounts and laughed and laughed until the buggy was out of sight.

A half mile further on, John Buchanan remarked to his wife that he had just seen Major McAulay go by the store as if he'd seen a ghost.

"More likely," she answered, "he's just seen Donald Morrison!"

Mac McLean

McLean found Donald and Norman eating a dinner in the kitchen of Finlay McLeod's Hotel in Spring Hill. Norman sat by the window and watched the road. Donald had his back to the wall. McLean walked in and began pulling money from his pockets right and left and scattering it on the table — drawing bills from his coat, his trousers, his shirt, one after the other and letting them fall like leaves about Donald's plate, narrowly missing the gravy.

"There," said Mac, making sure his pockets were all empty at last. "That is eight hundred dollars."

Donald looked up and awaited an explanation.

"Well, McAulay had a change of heart, so he did," said McLean, rubbing the back of his neck with a horny hand and keeping his eyes on Donald's plate. "Says he's not had a good night's sleep since he cheated you of your money and so he's paying it all back."

Donald glanced at Norman who grinned and shrugged. He squinted up at Mac McLean, took a mouthful of potato and began gathering the money into a neat pile. When it was all in, he handed it back to McLean.

"Send it back to them, will you?" he said. "Thank them very much from me but tell them it's my own money I'm wanting and not theirs. I can't be taking it."

"Them?" said Mac, his honest face working in all directions at once under Donald's smile. "But I said, McAulay . . ."

Donald grinned, "You are a very poor liar, Mac."

McLean protested to Norman who merely shrugged once more. He sighed, pulled out a chair and sat down astraddle. He munched morosely on a bit of Donald's bread.

"I told them it wouldn't work, so I did."

He told how the hat had been passed among the Companions of the Iron Stove in the hope that it was only eight hundred dollars that stood between Donald and his freedom. The Companions had gone off in separate directions with hats of their own and sugar bowls and mattresses were very soon up-ended from Mount Gosford to Weedon Lake. Letters went out and letters came back with enclosures. Even the detectives had been subtly touched for a donation. They were told it was for a poor homeless orphan.

"But I told them it wouldn't work," said Mac, again as he wistfully examined the pile of bills.

"I seem to have a great many friends," said Donald. He was genuinely touched by the gesture and sorely tempted but his mind was made up and he had to refuse. "Give them back their hard-earned money, Mac. Tell them I'm very grateful but I can't be taking it."

McLean turned to Norman.

"Can't you do anything with the man?"

"I've been trying for a week," Norman replied. "He has the hardest head in the county."

They finished their dinner while Mac stuffed the money back into his several pockets, distributing bills here and there according to a system of his own. Norman kept his eyes on the road.

"Look out," he said. "Here's Mrs. Finlay back from the store."

Donald jumped up and searched his pockets for coins. Police and detectives were one thing but Mrs. Finlay McLeod was something else altogether. She was a niece of Major McAulay and had no love for Donald or for anyone else for the matter of that. Finlay had sneaked them into his kitchen for a meal without her knowledge. He burst in all excited.

"Quick! She's back! Out this way! Quick, now!"

They followed him out through the side door and across the yard where the washing hung, hopped over a fence and reached the road. Norman stopped to catch his breath.

"Oh, it's an exciting life you lead, Donald."

Donald grinned and held out his hand.

"Forgive me for not coming to the station with you," he said. "I hear Carpenter has a man watching the trains."

"Good-bye," said Norman. "And good luck."

He turned back toward the station. Donald went off with McLean.

Major Malcolm B. McAulay

Major McAulay checked through his window every night to make sure his guard was at his post, slept with a revolver beneath his pillow and awoke each morning with a pain in his ear. His nerves were frayed. His temper was terrible. He was afraid to go anywhere without a bodyguard and his business consequently was suffering badly. Sherbrooke hotels were expensive. Constant vigilance was wearying. He had tried pressuring Carpenter for more ruthless action in bringing that outlaw to justice the way he had pressured Morin but Carpenter's temper was short, too. He kept a soft pillow on his office chair but still could not seem to get comfortable. He had simply given McAulay notice that he could not spare men to guard his house much longer and had summarily thrown him out.

It was time to beat a tactical retreat. The major decided to close up his residence and inform his neighbours that he was returning to Scotland for a few weeks on a matter of business. A bit of an estate left to him in a legacy or something. They should believe that. Then he could go to Cookshire where his men were constructing a sewerage system, live with his father-in-law and lay low until Donald Morrison was killed or captured.

Malcolm Matheson

Malcolm Matheson went across to see Carpenter, sat himself down on a chair with no cushion and dug for his pipe. He waited until it was well lit before he said what he had come to say.

"Chief," he began, "I've been thinking about that little chat we had in the store a while back."

"Yes?"

Malcolm puffed and deliberated for a good long moment.

"My apologies to your wife and kids and all, but I'm thinking this outlaw of yours is not likely to be leaving."

"And why not?"

Again Malcolm thought things over while filling the room with smoke.

"He belongs here," he said.

Pierre Leroyer

Carpenter had his answer. Donald would neither be driven from his home by police nor by promises and the citizens would continue to back him to the hilt. This answer called for another change of tactics.

His men had been probing here and there, wandering about, making sporadic raids and getting nowhere. It was time for a retrenchment. He set up a detective encampment in the woods not far form Marsden so that his men might more easily wait and watch Murdo's cabin and the home of Augusta McIver. He sent others to lie hidden at crossroads, hilltops, the approaches to settlements and villages and the order of the day was patience. Sooner or later, Donald would blunder into firing range. He took another trip to Montreal and, at his return, hired an experienced hunter to guide his men on occasional forays into the woods.

Pierre Leroyer was tall, dark, wiry and wore his hair cascading over his shoulders in the style of Buffalo Bill. He looked and behaved like an Indian or a halfbreed and was often called such although he had actually been born in Chateauroux, France. As a soldier, he had three times been wounded in the Franco-Prussian War of 1870-71 and then had hunted and trapped for the Hudson's Bay Company before settling down near Megantic. There he served as guide for the Megantic Fish and Game Club and lived in a cabin with four bears, two deer, a brace of monkeys and a porcupine.

This colourful character walked in on Carpenter one afternoon and offered his services.

"I 'ear you lookin' for a good guide, eh?"

"That's right. Are you Pete Leroyer?"

"You bet."

"Chief Hughes has mentioned you. He says you know your way about these godawful woods. That right?"

"I've 'unted and trapped these woods a long time, eh?"

"Right," said Carpenter, measuring his man and liking what he saw. He had the reputation of a remarkable shot and a tireless hunter and Carpenter was tired of his flatfoots getting themselves lost whenever they wandered out of sight of a road. Leroyer could lead them to places they had never been before, places where Donald Morrison might well be hiding.

"You're on," said the Chief. "I think I saw you once at the Winter Carnival driving a tame moose."

"You bet," said Leroyer with a broad grin. "Only man ever broke a moose to 'arness, eh?"

"Right," said Carpenter sourly, seeking a more comfortable position on his pillow. "You might be of use just the same." He bellowed for McMahon.

"This is Pete Leroyer, Jim. He's going to help us catch Morrison."

"Glad to have you with us," said McMahon. They shook hands.

"Take care of him, will you? He can pitch his tent out in the woods with your lot."

"Yes, sir," said McMahon.

The Reverend McLeod

Donald was staying once more with John Hamilton and learning the shoemaking business to pass the time. Avoiding the law was a temporary trade at best and cobblers were always assured of work. He had a mouthful of brads, a rubber apron and the good smell of new leather about him then when the Reverend McLeod came calling.

"Good morning, Donald," he announced. "We aren't seeing much of you in church these days."

"We aren't seeing much of you in the cobbler's shop, either," said Donald. "Those shoes are a disgrace."

"Aye," said the minister, morosely inspecting his feet. He was a long thin man with a great shock of white hair and a habit of chewing on his spectacles when he was thinking. He munched away now as he took a chair and studied Donald. "I heard you were wanting to see me on something."

"I was," said Donald and he laid a bulky envelope on the bench. "My friends are telling me that the Caledonian Society has shown some interest in my predicament and might be willing to help. They are saying you're the man who knows them."

"Yes. I have had some dealings with them in the past," said the minister. "It is a very worthy and worthwhile organization."

He replaced his spectacles and examined the envelope.

"I've gathered all the papers that have to do with my

troubles," Donald said, "and I'd appreciate it if you'd see they get in the hands of Mr. Blake."

"I'll do that and gladly."

"Thank you," said Donald.

The minister removed his spectacles and chewed once more.

"Will you not be giving yourself over to the police, Donald?"

Donald shook his head and picked up his hammer.

"I can't. Not yet. Maybe if the Caledonian Society sees their way clear to helping me out in the courts, then I might do it but not yet. Not now. I've no money and no hope for justice."

"Aye," said the Reverend McLeod. "These are troubling times for all of us, Donald." He watched the hammer for a moment. "How long will it take you to give me a good sole-and-heel job?"

Donald laughed.

"Better see the boss when he comes back," he said. "It might take me longer than I care to stay in one place."

And that Sunday, when the folk were all at service — coats and gloves and boots all steaming from the heat of the woodstove in the corner — the Reverend McLeod, still in his disreputable shoes, cleared his throat to announce a hymn when the door burst open to admit an excited Willie MacAuley.

"Is anyone knowing where Donald is this day?" cried Willie to the congregation. "I've just seen nine officers about two miles off and they are coming."

Donald MacRitchie was first out of his seat.

"He's at John Hammond's. I'll be warning him if someone'll give me a hand with the team."

There was a general exodus of men from the church as they grabbed coats and hats and ran out to help. The minister closed his mouth, lowered his white head and munched his spectacles while the women and children whispered excitedly one to another. The men in the snow outside helped MacRitchie back his team from the church shed and harness it to his sleigh. They saw him off and trooped back into church. The Reverend McLeod smiled softly down until all were reseated and the buzz of questions stilled and then he cleared his throat once more.

"We will now sing hymn number one-thirty-one," he announced. " 'Ride on! Ride on in Majesty!' "

MacRitchie rode on in haste and reached Donald a bare few minutes ahead of the law. They headed off, looked back from the top of a hill and saw John Hammond's house surrounded.

"That was a close one," said MacRitchie.

"Close enough," said Donald, quietly. "Look there."

A second group of officers had appeared suddenly on the road ahead of them.

"Just let the horses walk," said Donald. "Don't be hurrying."

MacRitchie did as he was asked although every nerve in him wanted to go like the wind. The officers halted and awaited their approach.

"Morning," said Donald, right out. "'Cold day to be out, so it is."

"We're after that damned Morrison again," said an officer with a very red nose who was stamping his feet to keep warm. "I don't suppose you'd be knowing anything about him, eh?"

"As a matter of fact," said Donald, "I heard he was to John Hammond's place just over the hill there. But I wouldn't be knowing that for sure. You know how rumours fly."

The officer flapped his arms and thought a moment. Even if Donald was not at Hammond's — which was more than likely — they'd at least be sure to get a cup of tea and a few minutes by the stove.

"I suppose we'd best go down and see," he said.

The other officers sat hunched on their sleigh muffled to the eyes and taking no interest at all in the talk.

"Good luck to you then," said Donald and MacRitchie clicked the team on. He heaved a deep sigh of relief and shot a sideways glance at Donald.

"Oh, you are a cool customer, Donald Morrison," he murmured.

Donald grinned. "Drive on, Mr. MacRitchie," he answered. "And don't be looking back."

"But you'll have to watch it," MacRitchie whispered. "You're about the only man in the country ever helps them in their hunt and someday they'll catch on."

"Hey! You two! Stop!"

MacRitchie was lifting his whip when Donald's hand restrained him. He didn't want his friend exposed to a shower of bullets. He pulled back on the reins and turned in his seat. The officer came running up behind them with a carbine in his hand. They sat still and waited.

His eyes flicked from one to the other.

"Either of you two spare a match?" he said. "Ours are all wet from the snow."

"Surely," said Donald. "Here." He handed over half-a-dozen from a tin box in his pocket while MacRitchie stared straight ahead and desperately wanted to do something with his hands. "You should be keeping them in a little tin box like I do."

"Much obliged," said the officer and he tipped his hat and stamped back to his men. MacRitchie stirred the horses but it was quite a while before he could bring himself to glance once more at his passenger. Donald was smiling at him.

They went on to MacRitchie's place but Donald wouldn't stay. He claimed it far safer to be one step behind the police than a mile in front and so he borrowed a pair of snowshoes and walked back through the woods to John Hammond's. The two parties of officers had met there, searched the place from cellar to attic, had a drop of tea and went on their way. They were well accustomed to failure.

"Well," said Hammond as Donald re-entered and hung up his hat, "this *is* a Sunday for visitors."

Augusta McIver

Augusta's father came in from putting the horses to bed and sat down to remove his boots. Augusta was helping her mother with the supper dishes.

"There's something hiding in the bushes just across the road," he said with a wink at his daughter. "Something keeping an eye on the house to see we don't get robbed. The old dog keeps running over to play with them, so he does. Thinks it's a game of Hide and Go Seek, I shouldn't wonder. Whenever he's getting too close, a size fourteen boot comes out of the bush and kicks at him!" He chuckled and Augusta smiled. Her mother laughed out loud. "Oh, he thinks it's great fun, so he does. He caught hold of a pant-cuff a while ago and was almost dragging an Indian into the road!"

He bent to get his boots off, chuckling and wheezing. When he straightened again his face was red and his tone more confidential.

"Augusta," he said, "I left my old snowshoes down at the sugar camp a while back and I'll be needing them come morning. Would you mind slipping down there before it gets too late and be fetching them for me?"

Augusta looked curiously at her father and he met her gaze full on with a twinkle in his eye. She understood in a rush and blushed as quick. "All right," she said and reached for her coat.

"Better slip out the cellar door," said McIver. "Don't want to be spoiling the old dog's game, do we?"

Augusta blushed once more and nodded and stepped into her boots.

"Be careful, dear," said her mother. "And don't you be staying too long, you hear?"

"I'll hurry," she said and she ran all the way to the sugar camp through the snow. It was cold and dark and terribly empty and there was no sound but her own panting. Then Donald was suddenly beside her with the light of the moon on his face and everything was just fine.

They didn't speak. They didn't touch. They merely stood smiling rather foolishly at each other for a long, long moment. He looked fit but a little tired and that was only to be expected the way he was hunted day after day with never a minute's safety or a moment's rest. His eyes and his smile, however, were just as bold as ever they were and she felt her colour rise and broke the silence.

"The police are watching the house," she said.

"I know," said Donald. They're having a high old time with that dog, eh?"

"Dad says there's an Indian with them."

"That's Pete Leroyer," said Donald. "He's a very good man, so they say."

"Yes," she said in a very small voice and then, "Oh, Donald! What are we going to do?"

He took her hands, then, and sat her down on a bench against the wall. He squatted down in front of her, still holding her hands in his.

"I can't be giving up just yet," he said. "I'd stand no chance in the courts of law and my only hope is to keep running and hiding a while longer. If I can get the Caledonian Society to help, there might be a chance for justice in the end."

She bit her lower lip and dropped her eyes. But what if you are shot down first? she was thinking. What if you are shot and killed? He reached out a finger and touched the tip of her nose. She smiled and sniffed and looked at him once more.

"But you," he said, "you are going away for a while."

Her face showed pain.

"Oh, no, Donald! No! I want to stay here. I want to see this thing through."

"You want to help me, don't you?"

"Yes," she said. "But, I'm not . . ."

"Then you must be going away for a while. There's nothing at all you can be doing here except get into trouble on my account and I'm not wanting that. Anyway, it's all arranged. Your father and I have talked it over and we are agreeing you should be going back to Boston for a time."

Her eyes misted over and she averted her face once more. She wasn't at all sure she wanted this man ordering her about and arranging her future as if he owned her but yet she could see sense in his scheme. He ran terrible risks each time he came to see her and the police might find a way to use her, sooner or later, as one more lever to pry him out of hiding.

"All right," she said at last. "I'll go. But please be careful, Donald."

"Don't you worry," he said and he kissed her on the tip of her nose. She held her breath as he drew her up, wondering if he were going to kiss her again and properly this time and wondering just what she should do about it if he did but he only said "Don't you worry" again and smiled and let her hands go. She wanted to hit him. She turned slowly to the door. She wanted to say good-bye but she couldn't trust her voice.

"Hey!"

She turned.

"You were forgetting your father's snow-shoes."

She snatched them out of his hands and ran all the way back to the house. He was the most aggravating man she had ever had the misfortune to meet and she just couldn't wait to get to Boston.

James McMahon

McMahon was a good detective. Whatever he might have lacked in imagination, he more than made up for in courage and tenacity. He had been born and raised on a farm near Sainte-Monique, Nicolet, and had joined the police only three years before. He was six feet two inches tall, broad-shouldered, ham-fisted and had already made a modest reputation for pluck and brawn by seizing runaway horses in the city and assisting Carpenter in the arrest of McGrath, the murderer. Now he and Leroyer were living in tents in the snowy woods near Marsden. They had spruce boughs and buffalo robes for sleeping and an open fire for cooking their meals. Their days were spent spying on houses, kicking at dogs or in searching the woods where they succeeded only in frightening a good many deer.

Occasionally, they raided places where they had reason to believe Donald might be sheltered. More often than not, their leads proved false but sometimes they were lucky.

While Leroyer watched outside, McMahon questioned old Mrs. Campbell as that lovely lady sat in her cabin by her bed and answered all his queries in the Gaelic. He asked if she'd seen Morrison at all and she invited him to have a drop of whisky against the cold. He couldn't understand a word of it and asked if she didn't speak a bit of English. "Pull your foot in a bit, Donald," she answered in her mother tongue. "I can see it sticking out from under the bed."

McMahon asked her to repeat that, slow and easy, and she obliged him, smiling up into his face all the while as Donald carefully removed his foot from view. McMahon gave up trying to understand anything she said and shoved his rifle under the bed. He reached an empty chamber-pot, probed no further and left the old lady rocking back and forth in peace. He never knew how close he had been to a three-thousand-dollar reward.

Or a bullet between the eyes. For Donald let it be noised about that he always had his pistols with him and would never be taken alive to hang. This had the effect of making the hunters over-cautious and affording him precious moments in which to get away.

McMahon led a party to Willie MacDonald's place on the North Hill. Willie, his son Dan, and Donald himself were seated at the kitchen table while Big Bob MacDonald, another son, was out in the barn attending a sick cow. When the dog began his clamouring and McMahon began his hammering at the door, Donald ran upstairs. Mrs. MacDonald put the kettle on. Old Willie scowled up from his Bible. Daniel unfastened the door.

"Come in," he said. "Come in and sit yourselves down. Will you be having a cup of tea?"

McMahon and his men came in all right but ignored any further invitation. Constables were sent to search the house from bottom to top, leaving wet tracks from their snowy boots all over Mrs. MacDonald's floors, while McMahon remained in the kitchen. Daniel showed him a revolver he had brought back from the west and asked his opinion about the piece, him being an expert and all. McMahon exhibited his Colt and proclaimed it a better weapon. Daniel absent-mindedly loaded his piece and argued over the comparative merits of hand-guns while old Willie recited a psalm in the Gaelic. The men returned from clomping about upstairs and reported finding nothing. McMahon led them out and elsewhere. Daniel unloaded his pistol and went on a search of his own.

Hearing the dog and spotting the officers, Big Bob MacDonald had sprinted up from the barn with a ladder. He guessed Donald would hide upstairs, propped his ladder against a second floor window, helped the man down and returned the ladder without anyone being the wiser.

Peter Matheson

Augusta left for an indefinite stay with her aunt and Donald was getting tired of running and hiding. He became depressed. His thirty-first birthday had been spent huddled under a pasture spruce in a driving snowstorm and Donald was a sociable man. He wanted a bit of light and laughter, music and singing and dancing and, by God, he was going to have it. He was heading for Spring Hill and a little private celebration when Mac McLean and Peter Matheson overtook him on a sleigh.

"What are you doing down here, man?" yelled Peter with great delight. "Are you not knowing that McMahon and the Indian have you trapped in a house up to Winslow?"

"I'm always the last to hear of these things," said Donald as he climbed up with a grin. "Is it bad?"

"You're completely surrounded," said Mac. "You haven't a ghost of a prayer of getting out alive."

"Ah, me," said Donald.

"I had it from a soldier," said Peter. "His horse dropped a shoe and he stopped at my brother's place, so he did. Seems McMahon and the Indian saw you go into the place and were keeping an eye on it until reinforcements arrived. Carpenter and his men went racing by not twenty minutes ago."

"They have me this time for sure, then?" said Donald.

"For certain sure," said Peter.

"Nice as pie," said Mac.

"Where are you off to, anyway?" said Peter.

"I was only on my way to Finlay's for a drink and a chat," said Donald.

"Bad luck," said Peter.

"He's away," said Mac. "The old battleaxe is minding the store and she wouldn't give us a cup of cold tea."

"Damn," said Donald. "I had a good thirst going, too."

"Likewise," said Peter. "Who do we know who's likely to have a bottle hid?"

"Finlay's isn't the only barroom in the country," said Mac McLean slowly and Donald looked sharply at him.

"Let us go to Megantic, then," said Donald.

"Megantic?" said Mac.

"The lion's den?" said Peter.

"Why not?" said Donald. "You just said yourself they were all to Winslow closing the trap."

"Then why are we wasting good drinking time?" crowed Mac McLean and set the sleighbells ringing on his team.

At Megantic, they marched right into the Prince of Wales Hotel, headquarters of the enemy.

"Set up the beer, Frank," said Donald. "It's been a very long and thirsty winter, so it has."

"You're crazy," said the bartender. "The police are in and out of here all the time."

"So you'd best be hurrying it up while they're out," said Mac.

"Oh, no," said the bartender. "You'll get nothing here. They'd lock me up for harbouring."

Donald eyed him steadily. Frank glared back. Peter Matheson came up with an idea.

"Are you carrying your pistols with you, Donald?" he asked, and winked.

"Surely," said Donald, pulling them out for all to see. "I always carry them for you never know when you might want to shoot somebody."

All three men smiled at Frank Legg and the glasses appeared like magic.

"That's the way, Frank!"

"Good old boy."

"Drink up and get out of here."

"Let us toast Major McAulay."

"Him with a grin like a crocodile."

"Sews his pockets up before he goes to bed."

"Does he now?"

"Keeps a lock on the outhouse door and fills his cake with sennapods. Rent you the key for a nickel."

"Dear old soul!"

"Fill them up again, Frank."

"Good boy, Frank!"

"I've a very appreciative throat this day."

They had a high old time in Megantic, laughing and singing right in the teeth of the manhunt. Each time a customer entered they bought him a drink, slapped him on the back and made sure he was aware that Donald had his revolvers handy. No one seemed inclined to leave after that, even when Mac started playing his harmonica and Mac's music, in the normal way, was enough to empty a graveyard.

"Give us another song, Donald."

"Give us a speech."

"A speech, man. Yes."

"Fellow sufferers!"

"That's the way!"

"Fellow sufferers, we are gathered here tonight to do justice to God's good grog!"

"Frank! Me glass is empty."

"Major McAulay, I understand, is a Teetotaller. Now, that's all right. I've nothing against Teetotallers but I'm a Presbyterian myself!"

"Good on you!"

"Drink up and we'll have another!"

"This one's for Carpenter and his darling detectives!"

"Who's got a song?"

Bundled up in the sleigh at last, passing a bottle for warmth and company, they let the horses take them back to Spring Hill while they sang sad and sentimental songs in the Gaelic. They only passed one vehicle on the road — a sleighful of glum and tired policemen heading back towards Megantic and all so wrapped up in blankets and robes that they spared no more than a glance at the huddled figures heading the other way.

"But that," said Carpenter when he was told of the escapade, "is the straw that broke the camel's back."

C. Aimé Dugas

It was obvious to all concerned that this bold defiance of the forces of the law could be allowed to continue no longer. It was now March of 1889 and the police were no closer to apprehending Morrison than they were at the time of the shooting of Warren fully eight months before. On the contrary, in spite of all their efforts, the fugitive apparently felt himself safe enough to march into the middle of Megantic in broad daylight, to drink and carouse at the very hotel that served as headquarters for the police and then to wander off singing. Such blatant contempt could not be endured. If the rule of law was to survive at all in this country, it was high time to put an end to the adventures of Donald Morrison.

There was another meeting of very important people. Carpenter and Chief Hughes of Montreal, Chief Moe of Sherbrooke, Attorney General Turcotte and Deputy Attorney General Fitzpatrick worked out an emergency plan that had the full and immediate approval of Premier Mercier. C. Aimé Dugas, Judge of Sessions and Extradition Commissioner, was given full and complete authority over a new expedition to capture Donald at all costs. He was provided a motley force composed of all available manpower — Quebec Provincial Police, Montreal City Police, jail guards and a new detachment of volunteers from a Quebec militia unit.

Martial law was declared in the district and anyone aiding and abetting the fugitive was subject to immediate arrest. "The utmost rigour of the law will be meted out to them," Dugas announced to the press. "They are well known to the authorities and can not escape. It is only a matter of time before they will all be lodged in the Sherbrooke Gaol."

Dugas arrived in Megantic at 11:30 p.m. on March 29th, 1889, just nine days after Donald and his friends had painted the town red. He was accompanied by his clerk, Dr. Tremblay, by his chief lieutenant, High Constable William Bissonette of the District of Montreal, and by Peter Spanjaardt, the go-getting young reporter from the Montreal *Star* who was in search of another interview with the outlaw and another scoop for his paper.

Dugas, next morning, set up a temporary headquarters in the Prince of Wales, consulted with Chief Carpenter and interrogated Frank Legg, the bartender. Legg mentioned Donald's display of his revolvers and the judge pounced. Obviously a threat to do bodily harm. Dr. Tremblay made out a deposition and Legg signed it. Dr. Tremblay made out warrants for the arrest of Mac McLean and Peter Matheson and Dugas signed them. Then Dugas sent for Malcolm Matheson.

The messenger returned a few minutes later with the word that Mr. Matheson was busy at the moment but would try to squeeze the judge into his schedule when he found the time.

Carpenter smiled. Dugas fumed. He simmered and spat like a kettle of soup and was on the point of issuing a third warrant when Malcolm sauntered in and sat himself down. The judge boiled over.

"Listen, Matheson," he roared, "I've a good mind to send you to jail right now!"

Malcolm brought out his pipe and examined the bowl, knocked the dottle on his boot, inspected it once more, took one or two experimental draws and then began a search for his black shag tobacco.

"Did you hear what I said?" cried Dugas. "Do you fully understand the seriousness of this situation? I have enough evidence on you to lock you away for a good long time and I am quite willing to do so unless I get some cooperation. The next time I send for you, you'd better drop whatever you are doing and come running. Is that clear?"

Malcolm unhurriedly tamped tobacco into his bowl, returned the pouch to his pocket and went searching for his matches. At last he cocked a blue eye at the judge.

"Your Honour," he said, "would you be having such a thing as a match about you?"

The judge leaped from his chair and stalked to the window, desperately trying to regain control of himself. Carpenter sat with his chair tilted against the wall and his hat tilted to the back of his head and suppressed a smile. Dr. Tremblay pretended to be very busily writing but his mouth was pursed with disapproval — he could see nothing amusing in disrespect for such an eminent personage as Judge Dugas. Malcolm had found a match, set his foul tobacco smouldering and was deliberately trying to fill the little room with smoke. The judge turned back from the window.

"You are suspected of aiding and abetting the outlaw Donald Morrison," said the judge, fixing him through his pince-nez, "by sending messages and supplies at various times to his place of concealment. What have you to say about that?"

Malcolm sat comfortably in his chair and measured his man through the smoke.

"This outlaw," he said at last, examining his briar, "what were you saying his name was again?"

The judge took a deep breath and that was a mistake. He coughed, he choked, tried to suppress it and choked again. Dr. Tremblay rushed up with a glass of water and overflowing concern for his master's health but the judge waved him off.

"Get that window open!" he gasped when the spasm had subsided and he was left with little more than a squeak in his voice and a stricture in his throat. He removed his pince-nez and squeezed the bridge of his nose.

He'd have to be very careful how he inhaled about Malcolm's black shag in the future for another such mistake might prove fatal. He caught sight of a twinkle in the storekeeper's eye and pretended to study the papers in front of him. They contained a report from Chief Carpenter concerning his suspicions of Matheson but there was really nothing in it that could be proven. A term for contempt might more easily be managed but that would make the man even less co-operative and the judge had need of him. He glared at the villain.

"I want you to know," he said evenly, with the full weight of his authority back in his voice, "that we intend to arrest every man who has aided and abetted this criminal in any form whatever." He paused. He stared down awfully. Malcolm's expression did not change. "Your own position in this matter is a most serious one." He paused again. "Every move you make from now on will be duly watched and reported to me." Once more, a pause. "Is that thoroughly understood?"

Malcolm understood that and more. He understood the judge was making use of Carpenter's method of spreading news throughout the community via Matheson's Companions of the Iron Stove. He intended to frighten the settlers into denying Donald any food or shelter while making Donald aware, at the same time, that he might be condemning his friends to jail whenever he accepted either.

Malcolm knocked the ashes from his pipe to the floor and stepped on them with a giant boot. The judge's relief at the cessation of smoke forestalled any remark he might have made about the spittoon in the corner. Malcolm got up and strolled to the door.

"Be a nice day if it don't snow," he said and was gone.

The judge sighed, took off his pince-nez and rubbed the bridge of his nose once more. It was going to be a long hard day. He sent Dr. Tremblay out to round up some sleighs to transport his party to Spring Hill and

Winslow and he asked Carpenter to bring in Mr. McLean, Donald's old advocate, who had requested an interview.

That interview went differently. The lawyer who had represented — or misrepresented — Donald during his troubles over the mortgage, was all too eager to co-operate with His Honour. He was a frightened man. Rumours had come to his ears that Donald Morrison had threatened to shoot him on sight. He had tried to shrug these rumours off, at first, feeling himself safe enough in Megantic with the police and detectives all about, but Donald's celebration had put the fear in him and he now asked for special police protection in return for telling all he knew of the outlaw, his friends and relations, the people of the settlements and the country itself. The judge pointed out that he could spare no men at the moment but would be glad to have Mr. McLean's company at their proposed headquarters in Winslow. His knowledge of Donald's affairs and of the district might be of some service. McLean accepted the offer.

Dr. Tremblay, meanwhile, had discovered sleighs were suddenly remarkably difficult to find. He would have supposed that almost every family in the village would have a sleigh for travel on the winter roads and that many would be willing to rent it out but wherever he went he met polite smiles and polite disclaimers. No one had a sleigh for hire. No one knew where he might discover one. He was beginning to fear the judge might have to walk those eighteen miles to Winslow when he stumbled on an old-fashioned three-seater that lay forgotten in somebody's barn. This served as transportation for His Honour, Bissonette, Dr. Tremblay, Mr. McLean and Peter Spanjaardt. Carpenter and his men, on instructions from the judge, remained in Megantic.

The party moved to Spring Hill. They stopped at Finlay McLeod's hotel for lunch and the judge questioned the hotelkeeper and his wife. Finlay admitted knowing the outlaw and boldly confessed providing him a meal in his kitchen. Mrs. McLeod claimed he was forced to it at the point of a gun. Finlay denied that was so. His wife insisted. Finlay protested. His wife abused. It made no difference and the judge sent them away to settle things in private while he signed another warrant for the arrest of Finlay McLeod.

Bissonette had been dispatched to bring in Peter Matheson and Mac McLean to answer the accusations in Frank Legg's disposition and to show cause why they should not immediately be thrown into jail. Neither could be immediately found. Willie Matheson, who would run from neither man nor beast, was discovered hard at work in his forge and conducted before His Honour covered with soot and grease. He knew nothing. He admitted nothing. He didn't even know where his brother could be found and had to get back to his smithy before the fire got down.

Dugas let him go with a warning to keep himself available. He pondered another arrest warrant but let it pass for the moment. There was little enough on Willie. He ordered Sergeant Leggatt and two constables to remain at Finlay's hotel to keep an eye on the blacksmith, the hotelkeeper, to locate Peter Matheson and Mac McLean but to do nothing further until receipt of instructions. The judge and his party bundled once more in the sleigh and jingled on to Winslow.

The hotel at Winslow was run by James Leonard and this was to be the permanent headquarters of the expedition. It was the geographic centre of Donald's range and a locality where he had often been seen. From North Hill, Red Mountain and Gould, Donald would have to pass either through Winslow, where the judge was waiting, or through Marsden, where detectives were encamped, in order to reach friends and relations in the south. Dugas had cut his range in two.

The judge invited Hugh Leonard, mayor of the town and brother to the hotelkeeper, to dinner and had a long discussion with him on the character and customs of the people. He learned that Morrison had been seen in Gould the day before and immediately sent Bissonnette and four officers in that direction. He sent a messenger to Marsden, telegraphs to Montreal and eventually retired for the night well pleased with his day. He had made his presence felt in the country and had impressed many people with the utter seriousness of his intentions. This was no longer to be a game of cops and robbers but a ruthless, single-minded manhunt. He was confident the settlers would no longer support the outlaw now that their own freedom was at stake and that Donald Morrison would soon be brought to bay.

Leonard's Hotel had never seen quite so much business. The little French-Canadian who was man-of-all-work about the place was running himself ragged trying to satisfy everyone. Besides Dugas and High Constable Bissonette, besides Dr. Tremblay and Mr. McLean, there were nine constables under a Sergeant Clarke and that young reporter from the Montreal *Star*. He hadn't near enough room to accommodate everyone even by doubling up. Spanjaardt, Sergeant Clarke and the constables had to sleep on the floor of the barroom rolled up in buffalo robes.

High Constable Bissonette

Bissonette — tall, lean, worn down to the bone by many years of dedication to the force, painfully polite and utterly ruthless — took his men to Gould in the night to capture Donald Morrison. At John Hamilton's house, Bissonette remained outside while Captain Giroux and three officers forced their way in, searched the place and pulled the shoemaker from his bed. He protested furiously at their methods and was told to shut up. Bissonette entered and sat himself down.

"Mr. Hamilton," he began, "I'm very sorry we had to disturb your rest but we understand you are a friend of Donald Morrison."

"Get out of my house."

"Do you know where we might find this murderer?"

"He is no murderer."

"We have information that he was here no more than an hour ago."

"Then your information's wrong. He left this morning."

"Do you know where he was going?"

"I do not."

"Do you know where we might find him?"

"Get out of my house and take your hooligans with you!"

"We have information that you sheltered him for a week."

"Then your information is wrong again."

"Two weeks, was it?"

"He was here no more than a couple of days. Now, get out and leave an honest man to his sleep."

"Thank you," said Bissonette. "You've been very helpful."

He led his men out and a message was dispatched to Winslow where another warrant was made out. The High Constable and his men moved on to search other houses and extract more confessions.

Sub-chief Lancy, in the small hours, was ordered to Spring Hill to pick up the officers there and press through the Middle District to Marsden and Scotstown. They were to search houses and interrogate suspects in the same heavy-handed fashion Bissonette was employing in the north. Dugas himself took to the roads in the morning and toured through Galson to Gould, from Gould to Scotstown, through Marsden to Spring Hill and so back to Winslow. He made his presence known and the weight of his authority felt in each of these communities and made certain the population knew of his expedition. His intention was to create such a stir in the northern and central parts that Donald would flee southward towards the Lake. There Chief Carpenter and his men were secretly lying in wait.

But Dugas did not yet know his fox. Donald, far from fleeing before the hounds, was hidden in a barn less than half a mile from Leonard's Hotel and keeping an eye on headquarters through a knothole in the wall. He even had a spy in the heart of the enemy camp — the French-Canadian general factotum about the hotel — who occasionally managed to sneak out with scraps of food and snippets of information.

Donald had left John Hamilton's in Gould with the intention of helping Murdock McLeod with his sugaring. Passing through Galson, he had been overtaken by a breathless schoolteacher who had spotted him from the window of her classroom and promptly deserted her students to warn him of the expedition. He listened quietly and thanked her kindly. He sent her back to her children, considered what he should do and decided to lie low near Winslow and learn what he could of this fresh government effort to trap him. Murdock would have to tap his trees without him.

C. Aimé Dugas

Dugas had more than one string to his bow. When Carpenter reported that Donald had either slipped through their net or had not been flushed from hiding, he immediately ordered the arrest warrants served on Finlay McLeod, Mac McLean, Peter Matheson and John Hamilton.

Finlay was arrested by his guests, Sergeant Leggatt and the two constables. He immediately closed the hotel, claiming his wife far too fragile to run it alone. This was a palpable lie, as anyone who had met that formidable woman could verify, but there was nothing the evicted policemen could do about it. They had to join their fellows on the barroom floor in Winslow.

Hamilton, the shoemaker, was picked up by Captain Giroux in Gould and Mac McLean was arrested when he showed up for work on the railway. Peter Matheson, having been warned by his brother, had taken to the woods and could not immediately be found but these three would do for a start. On Wednesday, April 3rd, just four days after the expedition had begun and proving the judge's statement to the press was no idle threat, McLeod, McLean and Hamilton were taken by train to Sherbrooke in the custody of Constables Beard and McKeown and locked in the Sherbrooke Gaol.

John McLeod

The settlers, far from being intimidated by these arrests, quickly devised a plan of their own to offset this new pressure. If a man left a packet of food on the kitchen table and forgot to fasten the back door before he went to bed, could he be blamed if some rascal sneaked in and stole that food? Of course, he couldn't. In fact, the blame must lie somewhere else and a man might just stop in and see that judge the next time he was in town and complain about the *dee*-plorable lack of law enforcement. Things were getting pretty slack when a man's own sandwiches weren't safe.

Others refused to compromise even this far. John McLeod was such a one. Bullying simply hardened his resolve and stiffened his resistance for he was Lewis-born, went in hard and kept on going. He was twenty-four, short and bearded. He worked on the railway and lived close to the station in Marsden. When he saw Donald walking down the tracks very early on the morning after the arrests, he went right out and invited the man in for a bit of breakfast. Donald accepted gladly and tucked into a plate of buckwheat pancakes with an enormous appetite. He had eaten nothing since leaving the barn in Winslow, had managed very little there and couldn't know when he might next come close to a bit of food.

John told him of the arrests of Finlay, Hamilton and Mac McLean. Donald put down his knife and fork and became very grave.

"I was afraid that would happen sooner or later," he said. He sucked maple syrup from his moustache and thought a moment. "Can you send a telegram for me, John?"

"I surely can."

"They might arrest you, too, if they catch you."

"Who is it for?" asked John, searching for a pencil and ignoring the remark as unworthy of consideration. Donald nodded and smiled.

"John Leonard in Sherbrooke. Hugh Leonard's boy. He's been letting it be known round and about that he's willing to offer legal advice whenever I'm needing it. I guess I'm needing it now. Tell him I'd like to meet him somewhere. Murdo McArthur's place might do but don't put that in the telegraph in case the detectives are reading them. Maybe you could meet him if he comes out and give him the word."

"Be glad to," said John and they discussed the matter for some time. As they were saying goodbye in John's backyard, the morning train pulled in from Sherbrooke and seven constables got off — more reinforcements to the battle front. Donald watched them for a few moments and then walked leisurely away while the officers fussed and grumbled over their baggage, stared at the surrounding woods and wondered where, in all this God-forsaken country, they would find Donald Morrison.

Mrs. Buchanan

Then Donald was trapped and he knew he was trapped. The police had somehow discovered he was on the North Hill and moved swiftly to cut off all escape. Bissonette led a detachment to Weedon on the Quebec Central Railway and moved carefully down from the north while a second group, under sub-chief Lancy, advanced up from Gould. Donald was trapped between. The snow was still deep in the woods but had begun to rot under the spring thaws which made travel next to impossible. He was caught between the jaws of a vice and the police were searching every house and barn, watching the woods for any sign of footprints and drawing inexorably closer. Donald was at the end of his rope. He determined to make a stand.

He wanted his friends to suffer no more on his account and had made them all promise they would raise no hand in his defence. He was on his own and would face it alone. They hated to leave him, knowing that he would be shot down like a mad dog and already seeing his red blood on the snow, but there was really nothing they could do to save him. The officers moved slowly in with rifles and side-arms at the ready. They met sullenness and hostile silence but the settlers kept their word to Donald and did not fight.

Donald recognized the approaching constables by the glint of the sun on their brass buttons. As they closed in for the kill, he drew steadily back. When the second force appeared behind him, he waded into the woods through knee-deep snow and got himself ready.

Mrs. Buchanan was alone in her house with the children when she saw Donald take to the woods. She stood at the window and chewed her nails. The police were coming and she had to do something. She slipped on her husband's boots, ran down the road and covered Donald's tracks as best she could. It was useless. No matter how she tried anyone with half an eye could see the snow had recently been disturbed just there and she returned disheartened to her home.

Sub-chief Lancy and his officers arrived in her dooryard. They searched her house and barn. They asked questions of her and the children but received no answers. They moved grimly on.

Mrs. Buchanan watched from the window in despair. Donald watched from the trees. The officers approached the place where he had entered the woods. Donald drew his pistols. Mrs. Buchanan gnawed at her nails. Incredibly, the police passed right by without a second glance at the snow. They met the party from the north and discussed the matter for some time. Donald could almost make out what was said. The first sleigh turned and headed back toward Gould with the second sleigh close behind. Again they passed right by Donald's tracks. Again they did not pause. Donald listened to the sleigh-bells jingling down the gathering gloom until he could hear them no more.

John Leonard

The Leonard family was strong in Winslow. They had come originally from Ireland but they spoke the Gaelic as well as Highlanders, pitched in with the rest and were eagerly welcomed by the Scottish pioneers. James Leonard ran the hotel. Hugh Leonard had been elected mayor. John Leonard, Hugh's son, had become a Sherbrooke lawyer.

He was more than eager to help the people of the settlements and met Donald, as arranged, at Murdo McArthur's place. Donald immediately asked news of the three prisoners in Sherbrooke Gaol.

"They are charged with harbouring a felon," said Leonard. "Finlay and Hamilton will probably be out very shortly but Mac McLean might have to stay a while longer because of that escapade in Megantic. They might bring a charge of assault or of threatening bodily harm against him because you exhibited your pistols. They could do that if they chose. They haven't found Peter Matheson yet or he'd be in the same fix."

"What are the chances of getting them out on bail?"

"Good. They have Broderick for a lawyer and he'll keep trying. I figure Judge Dugas will stall as long as he can to make an example of them but there will have to be a hearing sooner or later. The judge might then remand them in custody for eight more days but that's the limit under *habeas corpus*."

Donald walked up and down thinking hard and tugging on the ends of his moustache.

"I hate to think of them suffering because of me."

"They're all right," said Leonard. "Last time I saw them they were singing Gaelic songs and playing at cards. Finlay said to tell you it's the best holiday he's had since his wedding day."

Donald grinned. "Ah, that Finlay. He's a terrible man. A terrible man."

"But Judge Dugas is determined to catch you, Donald."

"I know it. He almost caught me on North Hill last night," said Donald. "It's a miracle that he didn't."

"What are your plans, then? You can't be running much longer."

"I've got to. I gave all my papers to the Reverend Mc-Leod a week ago and he's promised to send them to Mr. Blake of the Caledonian Society. I'm waiting to hear. There's talk of persuading the Government to let me turn myself in if the reward money is paid into a defence fund. I haven't a dog's chance otherwise."

"I don't think you need worry about your defence," said Leonard, stroking his own moustache. "You've no idea of the number of people who are on your side in this matter."

"I can't be taking charity," said Donald, marching again. "Too many people have suffered already on my account and Judge Dugas is going to keep it up, by the looks. And there's something else." He stopped and faced the lawyer. "I've been hearing rumours they plan to arrest my old father."

"Your father?"

"So I hear."

"Why would they do that?"

"They're out to get me any way they can, John, but you can't be letting them do it."

Leonard tugged on his ear and scowled. "I don't think they'll arrest the old man," he said, slowly. "But, if they do, I'm afraid there's no way I can stop them."

"But he's very proud and he's nearly seventy-seven," cried Donald. "I've been enough of a disgrace as it is but if they put him in jail, it might be the end of him."

"No. They wouldn't do that," said Leonard, shaking his head with sudden determination. "They're just trying to frighten you, trying to make you do something desperate."

"I hope you're right, then," Donald said bitterly. "Because I might just get desperate. If they lay a finger on that old man, after all I've put him through, I might just start firing these guns in earnest!"

High Constable Bissonette

Bissonette and his men pulled up outside old Murdo's cabin the very next day, quickly surrounded it and hammered on the door. Donald's mother opened to them, clutched her shawl to her throat and stepped backward muttering a prayer in the Gaelic. Bissonette entered without a word. Murdo sat in a rocking chair beside the window with his Bible on his lap and his glasses on his bald pate.

"Come in, gentlemen," he said. "Don't mind mother. She hasn't a word of English in her so if you've any questions, you'd best be asking them all of me."

Bissonette directed his men to search what there was of the cabin and pulled up a chair beside the old man. Sophie said something in her mother tongue and Murdo translated.

"She wants to know if you'll be staying for a cup of tea?"

"Thank you, no," said Bissonette who made it a rule never to accept hospitality while on the job. "This is strictly official."

"Suit yourself, then," said Murdo and shook his head at Sophie who sat down by the stove and nervously watched the constables go through her cupboards and drawers.

"Do you know where Donald is staying, Mr. Morrison?"

"I do not."

"When did you last see him?"

"I can't recall."

"When do you expect him?"

Murdo stared right back at him. "I would not tell you that."

"Do you expect him some time soon?"

Murdo said nothing.

"Do you understand that you can be arrested for aiding this man or for refusing to answer my questions?"

Murdo said nothing.

"Anyone suspected of offering food or shelter to your son is liable to immediate arrest and imprisonment."

"Our fathers and grandfathers fed people who were hungry," said Murdo, "no matter who they were and I'm hoping we will all be doing the same."

"I merely want to make it clear what yourself and all others risk by defying the law."

Murdo scowled. "Now let me be making something clear, Mr. Policeman. I've never yet thrown a man out of my house but if you and your men are intending to go on as you've begun, then, By God Almighty, I'll throw you all arsey-versey right through that window!"

Sophie was aghast to see such unnatural passion in her husband but Bissonette merely smiled and moved to consult with his constables. They had found a small locked trunk.

"Have you a key to this trunk, Mr. Morrison?" he asked.

"I have not," said Murdo.

"Break it open, then."

"Hold on there!" roared Murdo but one of the policemen stepped forward and prevented the fierce old man from charging from his rocker.

"I'm merely doing my duty, Mr. Morrison," said Bissonette. "Now you'll either sit quietly or I'll have one of my men handcuff you to the chair. Which is it to be?"

Murdo subsided, still scowling and black-faced with anger, and watched the policemen break the lock on Donald's trunk. They found clothes inside, ammunition, old letters and photographs.

"Take those letters and pictures along," ordered Bissonette. "And bring all the ammunition and firearms you can find."

"That's my hunting gun," roared Murdo, surging up once more. A burly policeman quickly stepped in front of him and laid a large hand on his shoulder.

"I'm sorry, Mr. Morrison," said the High Constable. "We are impounding all firearms and ammunition until your son is captured."

"You're all a scurvy bunch of thieves and robbers, then," declared old Murdo with great emphasis and went determinedly back to reading his Bible with one finger and the tip of his tongue. He didn't even see them out.

The High Constable and his men went out to their buggy, well satisfied with the raid. Dugas had considered the old man's arrest on some minor charge but decided such an outrage might steel the people in their resolve of non-cooperation while a raid might be just as effective in drawing Donald from cover. They next raided the Mc-Iver house, intending to bring the same sort of pressure on him through his sweetheart, but found Augusta long gone and safe from their bullying. They searched the place thoroughly — barns, waggon-shed, outhouses, sugar camp — but found no trace of the fugitive and none of his letters to Augusta. She had them all with her in Boston.

C. Aimé Dugas

Dugas pressed on. Sixty more men arrived bringing his total force to more than one hundred. These fresh reinforcements included another unit of volunteer militiamen under a Lieutenant Blouin, several Pinkerton detectives, more Provincial Police and jail guards. The police were armed with giant .48 calibre revolvers of the sort Warren once carried and the militiamen had Remington carbines or Snyder rifles. No expense was being spared in bringing Donald to justice and there were so many police and jail guards after him now that the Quebec Court of Queen's Bench and the Court of Special Sessions had repeatedly to postpone cases until their return.

A proclamation was issued to all Justices of the Peace and all peace officers in the district ordering them to assist in the manhunt in any way they could. Letters were sent out to all ministers of the Gospel asking for their co-operation. Search parties and road patrols continued day and night.

The letters and photographs Bissonette had found in Donald's trunk proved a valuable haul. Some of the letters were from Augusta McIver, postmarked Boston, and contained no confessions of a criminal nature, but others came from various citizens — Malcolm Matheson among them — giving detailed movements and descriptions of police and suspicious strangers. They proved complicity enough to keep Dr. Tremblay busy making out twenty-two new arrest warrants.

The photographs were even more interesting to the judge. He finally faced his victim for the first time.

"I'm delighted you came up with these, William," he remarked to the High Constable. "I was beginning to think the man a figment of some novelist's imagination."

Bissonette smiled.

"I was beginning to feel the same way myself," he said. "But he's out there. He's out there somewhere."

"We'll get him," Dugas replied, tossing the photograph to his clerk. "Have this reproduced and distributed with his description. We'll placard every tree in the country if we must."

"Yes, sir," said Dr. Tremblay. "And there are two gentlemen waiting to see you, sir."

"Gentlemen?"

"The mayors of Gould and Winslow, sir," said Dr. Tremblay. "I believe they are a delegation, sir."

"Hmm," said Dugas, removing his pince-nez and eyeing Bissonette. "What do you think they want, William?"

Bissonette shrugged.

"Perhaps I should leave and you can find out," he said.

"No," said Dugas. "You stay. You, too, Tremblay. Just show the gentlemen in."

Leonard and McMinn entered, were offered chairs and got down to business.

"We'd like to be arranging a bit of a truce."

"A truce?" snapped the judge. "This is not a war!"

"All right," said Leonard. "Call it what you like but we want you to call your men off long enough for us to be finding Donald and having a bit of a talk."

"What is there to discuss?"

"We think he might be persuaded to meet with yourself somewhere and be giving himself up if there's some guarantee of proper defence funds and no more arrests."

"The man is a wanted criminal. Why should I guarantee anything?"

"Because," said McMinn, "there might be blood otherwise."

"Not on my hands," Dugas retorted.

"Even a rat will fight if he's cornered."

Dugas thought it over. If he met Morrison privately and persuaded the man to surrender, it would be a feather in his cap for certain and put an end to the business. If he refused to attempt a meeting, he might stand accused later on of not doing all he could to avoid bloodshed. There could be no harm in trying. He would point out that nothing could be gained by further defiance, that he simply *had* to be caught sooner or later, one way or another, even if it meant arresting every Scotsman in the district. He simply *had* to be caught. No one could be allowed to set the entire judicial system of Quebec on its ear and get away with it for long. Such arguments, he thought, might do the trick if they came from a Judge of Sessions.

He cast an eye at Bissonette for his opinion and saw the High Constable nod almost imperceptibly.

"Very well," he said as he replaced his pince-nez and his judicial manner together. "I shall call the police off for forty-eight hours. You have my permission to arrange a meeting between Morrison and myself at a place of his own choice."

Privately, Dugas had yet a stronger reason for agreeing to the meeting. He wanted to see this man face to face. He conceded the man's courage and resourcefulness and was curious to discover what quality it was in him that made Donald such a determined adversary.

And, who knows? He might spot some weakness he could exploit later if he refused to give himself up. All men have weaknesses. That was the reason for law.

He notified Charles Fitzpatrick, Deputy Attorney-General, of his actions and of the proposed meeting. Fitzpatrick would inform Turcotte and Turcotte could tell Premier Mercier to let everyone know that Judge Dugas was not wasting time or the taxpayer's money. He postponed a hearing for the three prisoners in Sherbrooke Gaol and refused them bail once more. They could wait a few more days. He ordered his men to make no more arrests for the time being and sent more than half of them home on forty-eight-hour leave. Lastly, in case nothing came of the confrontation, he moved his headquarters to the small hotel in Gould and pressed an investigation of sympathizers and accomplices on North Hill and Red Mountain where Donald had made spectacular escapes. The total of arrest warrants in hand rose to forty-five.

John McLeod

Finding Donald proved no easy task. Since the arrests, since his last meeting with John Leonard, he had been keeping clear of his friends as much as possible. Nobody actually knew where he was but everybody knew where he might be and word went from house to house, people took to the woods, visited sugar camps and lumber cabins and empty barns.

The last time John McLeod saw Donald, after giving him breakfast in his house by the station, he had walked south along the railroad tracks. He had since been seen in both North Hill and Winslow but all the searchers in those quarters had so far come up empty-handed and there might still be a chance he had a hideout near the tracks. John borrowed a hand-car from the railroad and pumped his way slowly down the line from Marsden to Megantic, bellowing, every hundred yards or so, into the woods —

"Donald Morrison!" — and hearing only the woods bellow back — "Donald Morrison!"

Elsewhere, Augusta McIver's father was frightening the jays by bellowing in his own woods. Murdo McArthur looked in his cellar. Mayor Leonard, John MacIver and Mayor McMinn each patrolled separate roads but none found a trace of Donald.

The forty-eight hours was almost up. McMinn went back to the judge and asked for more time.

"I think you've had quite long enough to locate the man," answered Dugas, self-righteously.

"The police," said McMinn, "have been looking for nearly a year without a clear sight of him yet."

Dugas fiddled with his pince-nez. He really wanted this meeting but he could not appear too eager.

"What difference could a couple more days be making?" asked the mayor of Gould.

"You have another twenty-four hours," said the judge. "If this criminal is not located by then, our arrangement is cancelled."

As it turned out, they had no need of the extension. John McLeod had pumped his hand-car north from Marsden, still giving his whoop at the woods — "Donald Morrison!" — until the woods answered back — "What are you wanting?"

"Where are you hiding, you rascal?"

"Right here, John," said Donald, emerging from the trees quite close by. "What's all this hullooing about?"

In his usual audacious manner, Donald had been living less than a mile from the detectives' encampment at Marsden while they had been searching the remotest corners of the country.

"Judge Dugas has declared a truce on you," John said. "He wants to meet you somewhere to be having a bit of a talk."

"Whose idea?"

"Hugh Leonard and McMinn thought it up. You get

choice of time and place."

Donald sat down on the hand-car.

"Treachery?"

"We can make sure first."

"What do they want me to talk about?"

"Surrender terms. Money for your trial. A lot of prominent people think it is time you were giving yourself up."

"Mr. Blake?" said Donald. "The Caledonian people?"

"Not them," said John. "Not yet anyway."

"I suppose they're worried about more arrests."

"Maybe that," said John. "But I think it is your own welfare they're thinking on."

Donald tugged his moustache and sighed. He was getting very tired of running.

"All right," he said. "Tell them I'll meet him at the Galson schoolhouse. I've a friend there who will tell me if anything's afoot. Say five o'clock on Thursday. That's the eleventh, I think. One man on each side and no guns. Will you come with me, John?"

"I will," said John McLeod.

"Thanks," said Donald.

"I'll pass the word." John stood up and caught hold of the pump. "I'm getting awful tired of pushing this thing up and down," he said.

"One more thing, John," said Donald. "I'd like to be seeing that reporter again."

"Peter Spanjaardt? He's at Gould with the judge."

"Maybe you could send him a message for me."

"But that's the enemy camp," said John. "How'd it be if I sent a wire to Hugh Graham in Montreal and let him set it up with Spanjaardt? They wouldn't be as suspicious of a wire from his head office."

"That's a good idea. You'd make a good burglar, John. You've got a very devious mind."

"It's done," said John. "I'll set up both meetings. Now, don't you go getting yourself lost again."

"Me?" grinned Donald. "I knew where I was." And he

thanked his friend again and watched him pump his way back towards Marsden.

Peter Spanjaardt

John McLeod sent off his messages. Mayor McMinn informed the judge that Donald had been found and the meeting arranged for Thursday afternoon. Dugas asked where it would be but McMinn would not say.

"John MacIver will pick you up and take you there," he said.

The judge permitted himself to smile.

"You don't trust us, do you?"

"I'd trust you with my life, Your Honour," said McMinn, "But this life isn't mine."

"I'll be there," said Dugas. "Just make sure I'll not be wasting my time."

Peter Spanjaardt received a curious telegram from his head office written in a semi-cipher. It stated that if he should take the train from Scotstown to Marsden, he might there learn something of interest from "a small man with a large beard." Spanjaardt hopped a horse and raced to Scotstown immediately, for there was nothing he loved more than intrigue. He had stuck close to Judge Dugas ever since their arrival at Megantic but His Honour had little use for reporters and kept most of his activities strictly secret. Nevertheless, Spanjaardt had been filing stories every day, sometimes twice a day, on what he could pry from the officers, figure out for himself, or gain from interviews with the settlers. He continually dreamed of another interview with the outlaw and this was his first solid lead. He took the train to Marsden and there was met by John McLeod.

John looked him up and down and asked for identification. He asked questions about his first interview with Donald to be sure the man was who he represented himself to be and not some spy of the police.

"Fair enough," he said at last. "I reckon you are the right man. Let us be taking a walk in the woods."

"I'm afraid I'm not much of a woodsman," said Spanjaardt. "I get lost on Mount Royal."

"It's just to be making sure we're not followed," said John. "You can hear those big-foot detectives crashing through the brush half a mile behind. Are you carrying a weapon?"

"No," said Spanjaardt and his companion nodded. He had one of his own and might just be using it if need be but he did not say so. Instead, he led the reporter a long roundabout way to a woodcutter's shack that was actually little more than a hundred yards from Murdo Morrison's cabin and right in the heart of the detective's territory. They had a bit of supper there, waited until dark, and then Spanjaardt was led to the centre of a large field and left alone with his thoughts.

Within a few minutes Donald and another man rode up in a buggy. Donald jumped down and extended his hand.

"Good to see you again, Peter," he said.

The buggy was driven a little distance away and the two men talked.

"I asked for this meeting," said Donald, "to be getting my position across to the people again. I know I can be trusting you, Peter, and this might be the last chance we have for a bit of a talk."

"I'll do my best by you," Spanjaardt said.

"I know you will." Donald seemed depressed and tired. He kept passing his hand over his eyes. "This meeting with Judge Dugas; I've agreed with it only to please my friends but I've little hope. Nothing will come of it. I'll not surrender without some sort of justice from Major McAulay and the judge can't guarantee that. Then, if they're letting me back to the woods, they'll be hunting me down soon for sure. It won't be long, now. I hear there's more arrest warrants waiting to be served and I can't be getting any more of my friends in trouble."

"The last I heard there were forty-five warrants," said Spanjaardt.

Donald was shocked.

"That many, eh?"

"So I hear."

"Can they really be arresting that many, then?"

"I think they might," said Spanjaardt. "There's a lot of political pressure on Judge Dugas."

"But they're picking them up for bad reasons," said Donald, rubbing his eyes again. "Finlay McLeod, for instance. I only had but one meal from him and paid for it, too, but I was bound to have that meal and he couldn't have stopped me. It's not right."

He stroked his moustache and studied the stars. Spanjaardt was silent.

"I don't blame the policemen," he continued after a moment. "And I don't blame the soldiers, for they're only doing their jobs after all. It's those detectives. They're forever skulking about in the dark looking for a chance to kill me. I'm afraid I might be shooting one of them if ever I get close enough. That trunk of mine — they broke it open and took love letters and everything. I might have knocked a few down, then, if I'd been there."

Again he looked up at the stars and around to the shadows of the encircling trees and his expression was, for a moment, wild and desperate like that of a trapped animal. He had been hunted for eight full months. The strain was tearing him apart but when he faced the reporter again he was calm once more.

"So tell the people," he continued, "tell them I'm as strong and determined as ever I was. You can say from personal experience that I'm approachable to my friends. My enemies, I think, will not be taking me alive. *Soiridh*, Peter. I'm afraid we won't be meeting again."

They shook hands and Donald strode to the waiting

buggy and rode away. Spanjaardt remained where he had been left, mulling over the words and impressions he had been given and writing his story in his mind. He stayed too long and nobody came to lead him back to Marsden. He tried it alone but could not find his way through the ring of woods and blundered about in the dark until morning.

He filed his story, then, and returned wearily to Gould. When Judge Dugas left for his meeting at Galson schoolhouse that afternoon, he gave orders that Peter Spanjaardt was to be detained in the hotel — by force if necessary. He wanted no one talking to Donald but himself. He had no way of knowing the reporter had already scooped him.

Galson

On the afternoon of April 11th, 1889, Judge Dugas and John MacIver, a well-to-do farmer from the area, arrived at Galson schoolhouse for their meeting with Donald. It was a square, two-storey clapboard building with an excess of windows and a paucity of paint. The entrance hall doubled as a cloakroom and smelled of wet rubbers and mittens. The large classroom downstairs smelled of ink, woodsmoke, soap. An oil lamp had been left burning for them.

"It's been a long time since I was at school," said MacIver.

"See if you can get a window open," grunted the judge to forestall any nostalgia. "Let some air in here."

The judge walked up between the desks to the front of the room where a portrait of Queen Victoria hung over the blackboard. He took the chair behind the teacher's desk, sat down and looked around. Yes. That was the only place in the room for him. The desk stood on a raised platform and afforded psychological advantages well known to a judge. Donald would either have to stand before him like a prisoner in the dock or sit at one of the desks — ridiculously too small — and listen like a disgraced schoolboy. Either way, Dugas ruled the roost.

MacIver had a window open and sat on a wooden bench beside the iron stove. Someone had thoughtfully kept the fire going after class was dismissed and the room was quite warm. They waited in silence. The wall clock already indicated five minutes past the hour of their appointment. The judge picked up a pen and tapped it on the desk in time with the brass pendulum.

"What if he doesn't show up?" asked MacIver.

"He will," said the judge.

It was all to Donald's advantage. He had nothing to lose and everything to gain by this meeting and he was no fool. He had obviously picked the schoolhouse so no one could be charged with harbouring. It was neutral territory and further proof (if any were needed) that Donald was nobody's fool. Right now he was probably making them wait his pleasure for the same reason the judge had chosen to sit at the teacher's desk — psychological advantage. Dugas would be doing the same, now that he thought of it, and using the delay to make sure no treachery was afoot: no officers hidden in the woods or moving down the roads to block his escape.

The clock indicated ten minutes past the hour of their appointment. Dugas took out his watch and found the wall clock was four minutes slow. This was over-doing things a little. MacIver sat against the wall cleaning his fingernails with a pocket knife. The judge tapped his desk.

The classroom door opened without warning and two men walked in. The first was a tall man with a square jaw, blue eyes and a large moustache. The second was smaller and sported a full beard. The first strode straight to the front of the room, mounted the platform and sat on a corner of the desk. He looked down at the judge and held out his hand.

"I am Donald Morrison," he said.

By sitting so casually on the edge of the desk, Donald had immediately overcome the judge's attempt to belittle him and, by holding out his hand, had offered forgiveness. It was the judge who had to rise to politely take the proferred hand.

"Judge Dugas," he announced gruffly and sat down again to reorganize his plans. Things had begun all wrong.

"And this," said Donald, "is John McLeod."

McLeod nodded and went over to the bench where MacIver was sitting. He offered him the makings of a cigarette and the two rolled and smoked in silence.

The judge felt a need to do something with his hands and reached once more for the pen but Donald had already picked it up and was chewing on the end. Dugas, forestalled again, pushed back his chair and abruptly stood up so the man did not tower over him so. He paced up and down in front of the blackboard and below the portrait of maternal dignity.

"Morrison," he began, sharply, "I am here to offer you one last chance to give yourself up."

Donald smiled and chewed his pen.

"You will be given a fair trial and your voluntary surrender will count heavily in your favour. The charge, and I have this on the authority of the Attorney-General, will then be manslaughter in the shooting of Lucius Warren and all else — resisting arrest, threatening bodily harm, arson and assault — all the rest will be dropped."

"Will that get my farm back?" asked Donald.

"On the other hand," the judge continued sternly, refusing to have his speech side-tracked, "on the other hand, should you continue resistance to lawful arrest, matters can only go harder for you in the long run. I can fill these woods with armed men if necessary and it will only be a matter of time before you are either caught or killed."

He stopped on these last words less than a yard from

his adversary and glared into those cool blue eyes. Morrison stared as steadily back. The clock ticked.

"All right," said Donald softly. "Now you've had your say and you will kindly be sitting down and letting me have mine."

He waited, unmoving. The judge hesitated, but he could not help but admire the man's coolness and so drew out the chair and sat obediently down.

"Firstly," said Donald, "I'll be telling you my story because you may not have been hearing it right." He got up and paced in his turn before the blackboard. "I am guilty of shooting through a window and destroying a perfectly good clock and I'm sorry for that. I am guilty of frightening Madame Duquette and I'm sorry for that, too. My fight was not with her. I'm also guilty of threatening Malcolm B. McAulay and I'll do that again if I'm seeing his swindling, miserly, ugly red nose on this side of the Atlantic. He stole my farm and threw my old parents out into the road. The law backed him up every step of the way. That's the truth and so it is. But," he said, pausing in his march, "I have burned no barn and I have burned no house. I was ten miles away at the time it happened."

"Who did it, then?"

"How should I be knowing that?"

"But, after your threats, anyone burning that house and barn would know the blame should fall on you."

"I'm not saying anyone did it."

"How then? Does a barn set light to itself?"

"Could be," said Donald. "Spontaneous combustion. A man puts in a bit of hay that's not quite dry, puts a bit more on top and, what with the weight and the lack of ventilation, fermentation starts and the hay heats up. You take a bit off the top one day and — poof! There's your fire. Happens all the time. I could show you a dozen barns that were lost like that and sometimes they took the house down with them when the wind was right."

The judge considered and nodded. "That makes sense

except for one thing. There would be little hay left on the thirtieth of May."

"Try it the other way about, then," said Donald. "Could have been a chimney fire in the house. The old lady got a good hot fire going for supper and it got out of hand and took the barn with it. That happens, too. Could have been lightning, a bit of carelessness with a lantern or a match. Could have been kids smoking on the sly or an old tramp, maybe, wanting a warm place for the night. Whatever it was, I had nothing to do with it."

"You're not on trial here," said the judge.

"I'm telling my story," said Donald and resumed his pacing. McLeod and MacIver smoked and softly discussed the fishing. The clock ticked on.

"I am also guilty," Donald continued, "of killing Jack Warren. I did not want to do it and had no intention of doing it but it happened. I tried very hard to stay out of his way. Lots of people will be telling you that. When it came right down to it in the end, I had no choice. It was self-defence."

The judge clamped his pince-nez on his nose and snorted.

"Killing a deputized officer of the law who was attempting a lawful arrest can never be self-defence."

"I agree."

The judge removed his glasses and frowned. Donald watched the toes of his pacing boots and let him puzzle a moment before explaining.

"Warren was not out to arrest me. He was out to shoot me."

"How can you prove the man's intentions?"

"Maybe I can't be proving it. Not in your courts of law, anyway, but he intended to shoot me none the less. I could see it in his eyes. He was several times heard boasting that he would blow my head off. When he put up that target behind the hotel, he was practising shooting, was he not? He was not practising *arresting*."

The judge nodded and permitted himself a smile.

"You have spies everywhere, it seems."

"Friends," retorted Donald. "It is you who have spies."

The judge still smiled.

"Nevertheless, Chief Carpenter claims your intelligence system was often as good as his own."

"Better," said Donald and this time he returned the smile.

"All the same, Warren was a deputized officer. He was authorized to shoot only in self-defence."

"A man like that could not be trusted and you are knowing it. He should never have been deputized in the first place. The law just gave him an excuse to build his reputation by killing me and that's just what he was intending. I was lucky enough to kill him first and that, your Honour, is self-defence, be he deputized or not."

"I'm not sure the law would agree with you on that point."

"That's no surprise. The law never agrees with me. It backed McAulay on the mortgage. It got me fined for cutting up telegraph poles and let McAulay off for breaking down my door. The law deputized Warren. The law bullied my old father, stole my love letters, arrested my friends, hounded me all over the country. The law, sir, is a ass!"

The judge cocked an eyebrow.

"An outlaw quoting Dickens?"

"Outlaws have a lot of time for reading."

He resumed pacing and studying the toes of his boots.

"I may take it, then," said Dugas, adopting his official manner along with his pince-nez, "that you are refusing to surrender."

"You may," said Donald. "I'll not surrender until there's a chance of justice and there's no justice in your courts for a man like myself. It is no more than a game to see who has the best lawyer and that's always the man with the most money. Right now, I haven't a red cent. Mc-

Aulay's got it all. When he stood up in court that day, any fool could see by his face that he was guilty."

"The courts do not judge a man by his face."

"No. Maybe they should. All I know is a poor backwoods Scot like myself hasn't a prayer of justice."

"I'd remind you that Major McAulay is also a Scot."

"So was Monteith but we don't brag on it."

Again the judge smiled in spite of himself for he recognized Monteith as the man who betrayed William Wallace to the English. And he was beginning, now, to understand the quality of the man he had to deal with. He was stubborn and determined, surely. He cared nothing for the rule of law but, just as surely, he believed in right and wrong. He had a strong sense of justice inherited by hundreds of years of honest Scotch forebearers, a sense that saw things all in simple terms of black and white, right and wrong, and all his prattle of lawyers and courts of law was simply bitter disappointment that Old Testament values meant little in the field of jurisprudence.

And Dugas, no matter what his own feelings were on the matter, recognized this belief as a weakness that might be exploited.

"Then I have no choice," he announced with his gravity restored. "We have many new warrants ready for execution. The charges are of harbouring a felon which is a felony itself but, should you shoot and kill someone in your continued resistance to arrest, those charges might well become accessory to murder."

He glared at Donald. Donald glared back. The clock ticked.

"I'll shoot no one," he said at last and with a terrible weariness.

"But I, on the other hand, must fill these woods with armed men ordered to shoot you on sight."

"Yes," said Donald bitterly. "And that gives me no choice either. My friends would not be respecting me if I gave in to your injustice and I couldn't be respecting myself, either. I'd sooner be shot on the run than hanged for a crime I did not commit. I'd sooner be shot dead than spend the rest of my life in some stinking jail."

Judge Dugas rose from his chair with immense dignity.

"Good-bye," he said.

He did not extend his hand.

"*Soiridh!*" said Donald with defiance. McLeod was already checking outside. He stuck his beard back in and signaled to Donald that the coast was clear and they both slipped out to the darkness. When Dugas and MacIver emerged a few moments later, they had faded already into the woods.

John McLeod

The truce was over. Each knew where the other stood and there would be no quarter. John McLeod, the small man with the large beard, was arrested very early the next morning. He had been expecting it and did not resist. Willie Matheson was picked up at his smithy and they would have taken Peter, too, had they known where he was hiding. They arrested Murdo McArthur of Winslow, Murdock McAulay and Murdock McLeod and charged all five with harbouring. They were taken by train in the custody of Sergeant Clarke and Constable "Tall" McKeown and joined their three friends in Sherbrooke Gaol.

Finlay, Mac and John Hamilton had finally had their preliminary hearing. They had been brought before Messrs. A. G. Woodward and Israel Wood, Justices of the Peace, and were officially remanded in custody at the request of Judge Dugas. Broderick requested bail once more. John McIntosh, Member of Parliament, came forward with personal bail bonds of $1,000 for each of the three men but Judge Dugas insisted bail be refused. It was, he informed Broderick, "in the interests of your clients."

The truce was over. Donald had refused to surrender. Dugas had to get tough and there was scarcely a man in the district who was not expecting momentary arrest. Eight were now in jail but fifty more were quite ready to join them rather than turn against Donald. The judge, however, would make no martyrs. He decided that these arrests were sufficient for the time being and let the others sweat for a while — knowing that there was nothing like time for turning adventure to boredom. He reorganized his forces into groups of five men each. These were posted on the Marsden Road, at Spring Hill, North Hill, Red Mountain and Marsden itself. He considered a plan to use bloodhounds in the woods, left High Constable Bissonette in charge and journeyed to Montreal to consult with Fitzpatrick and Turcotte.

Mr. McLean, the advocate, had wanted to leave Winslow for some time but was afraid to travel without an armed escort. He was still under the impression that Donald intended to kill him. Bissonette had found him more a hindrance than a help to the investigation and was as eager to be rid of him as he was to leave. Constable Gordon, in full uniform and carrying a loaded carbine, accompanied McLean on the stage to Sherbrooke.

The truce was over. The foxhunt ran on.

Donald MacRitchie

The foxhunt ran on, over hill, over dale, into the woods and out again. While the hounds sniffed here, the fox lay there — watching from a covert or a window or a knothole in the wall of a barn. When the hounds searched there, the fox was here once more. He sometimes ran ahead of the hounds but more often followed behind at his leisure. Occasionally, he even joined them.

A party of officers stood in the road one night surrounded by settlers and all discussed the hunt in progress and wondered just when and where their quarry might be unearthed. At the edge of the circle, listening with polite interest, stood Donald himself.

He visited McFadden's store at Bishop's Crossing one cold afternoon with Donald MacRitchie and Angus McLeod. Several travellers sat around the stove discussing the hunt and wondering aloud what was the matter with the police that they had not yet captured this outlaw. They had his description and they had his photograph but they never seemed to recognize their man. It was just too much to believe, they said, and Donald, warming his hands over the stove, heartily agreed with them.

The MacRitchies never wavered in their support of Donald and always had a welcome for him in their home. John and Donald MacRitchie, both in their late teens, helped the outlaw out of tight corners again and again. It was Donald MacRitchie who had raced on his sleigh from the church to John Hammond's door and it was he again who spotted a party of officers approaching from the south when Donald was expected down from Red Mountain in the north. He ran across the fields and intercepted Donald on the road ahead of them. He told him to get in the woods quick for the police were right behind and then he hurried on up toward Red Mountain. The officers spotted him on the road ahead and raced in pursuit. They overtook him, stopped and questioned him closely. He claimed to know nothing of the outlaw but kept glancing apprehensively up the road toward the mountain as if expecting him at any moment. The officers were convinced. They put him under guard, hid their horses and waited for hours in the bushes.

Donald, meanwhile, had come out of the trees and was comfortably drinking tea at the MacRitchie homestead.

J. N. Greenshields

J. N. Greenshields, of Messrs. Greenshields, Guerin and Greenshields, had business at the Excelsior Copper Mines in Broughton, sixty miles north of the hunt. There had been a rumour — as there were rumours everywhere — that Donald had been seen working in the mines, and Greenshields jokingly mentioned to the telegraph operator that three men had gone down the Kent Shaft and only two had returned. "Could be," he said, "that third man was Donald Morrison."

He returned to Sherbrooke and thought no more of his chance remark until he received a desperate telegraph from the mine supervisor saying that Bissonette and four constables were demanding to search the Kent and Fanny Eliza Shafts and threatening prosecution if this permission were denied. "Let them go," Greenshields answered. "But warn them of the danger."

He meant the danger of wandering about underground but if they cared to interpret it as meaning the danger of meeting a crack shot in a narrow tunnel, that was their business. He was, nevertheless, convinced that they might search the mines for a month and find no trace of Donald.

But it was an indication of a new desperation on the part of the police that they ran down every stray rumour — even if it were sixty miles from Donald's territory and 1,600 feet underground. And it was an indication of the old audacity on the part of Donald that he was, at that time, hiding once again in the barn close to Leonard's Hotel and watching activities through a knothole.

The Associated Caledonian Societies

On Thursday, April 18th, Dugas returned to Sherbrooke and had all eight of the prisoners brought before him. Finlay, Hamilton, Willie Matheson and Murdock McLeod were all released on their own recognizance. Mac McLean, Murdock McAulay, John McLeod and Murdo McArthur were released on bail bonds provided by John McIntosh, M.P. Finlay, Mac and Hamilton had been in jail for sixteen days, the others for six. They went home on the evening train to a hero's welcome and the pipes wailed on into the wee hours of the morning.

Few thought to question the judge's sudden magnanimity in letting all his hostages go but those who did noted that Bissonette had received a visit from two representatives of the Associated Caledonian Societies that same day. Doctor Graham and Captain Richardson of Richmond, guided and accompanied by the Reverend McLeod, presented their authority in a letter from the Premier himself. Bissonette read it quickly, aware already of the message it contained, and turned to the delegation.

"I am at your disposal, gentlemen," he said. "Tell me what I can do."

Dr. Graham answered. "We bear a letter," he said, "from the Honourable Mr. Blake to Donald Morrison. If you would be so kind as to declare a moratorium, we should like to contact this man, arrange a meeting and acquaint him with the terms Mr. Blake has presented."

"May I know those terms, gentlemen?"

"Of course. They are not secret. Mr. Blake assures Mr. Morrison that the Associated Caledonian Societies will guarantee all the expenses of his defence if he surrenders himself to us."

"I see," said Bissonette. "And do you think he will accept?"

"We have every reason to believe so," said Dr. Graham. "It is all he has asked for."

Bissonette examined this delegation. Dr. Graham was a rather quaint, old-fashioned gentleman and Richardson a military man who had declined a chair and remained standing as stiff as a post. He had already met the Reverend McLeod with his great shock of white hair who was sitting a little behind the others and munching on his spectacles. And he already had his instructions from Judge Dugas so there was really nothing to discuss but the details.

"When would you like this truce to begin?"

"Tomorrow is Good Friday. We think it would be a Christian gesture if mercy began at dawn and lasted until such time as we have met with Mr. Morrison and received his answer."

Bissonette tugged at the lobe of his ear.

"Our forces are scattered," he said slowly. "It will take some time to inform all of them. It would be a more secure truce, I think, if I give orders tomorrow for it to begin on Saturday morning. Would that be agreeable, gentlemen?"

Dr. Graham looked enquiringly up at Captain Richardson who stiffly nodded.

"It would," said the doctor.

"And, instead of leaving it open, I will give you three days with the understanding that if you need more time, you have only to ask for it. That will be until midnight on Easter Monday. I can issue seventy-two hour leave to some of the men and let them visit their families."

"Excellent," said Dr. Graham.

He stood up to take his leave but the minister of Gould had a word to say.

"One more thing," said the Reverend McLeod. "We'd like to be having Chief Carpenter withdrawn from Marsden while this truce lasts."

Bissonette glanced sharply at the man while his mind raced through everything that might have prompted that request. Was it simply a cautious distrust of Carpenter's undercover tactics? Was the meeting to be in Marsden?

Was Donald hiding there right now and the minister aware of it? Did he have reason to suspect treachery?

The minister blandly smiled and chewed his glasses. Dr. Graham and Captain Richardson were waiting.

"Agreed," said Bissonette and it was all arranged.

He gave leave to all but sixteen of his men – a skeleton force in case of trouble. He sent Constable Giroux to bring Carpenter from Marsden to the Winslow Hotel and then Bissonette himself left for a weekend with his family in Montreal.

The Reverend McLeod next led the Caledonian representatives to a meeting with the mayors of Gould and of Winslow where they discussed how they might best locate Donald, notify him of the truce and arrange a meeting. Good Friday saw messages carried from house to house the length and breadth of the country. Volunteers went once more into the woods and to sugar-camps, woodcutter's shacks, remote farmhouses and empty barns. Once again the woods and hills rang with the call for Donald Morrison. Once again, it proved no easy task.

Carpenter arrived at Winslow on Saturday morning but he did not come alone. Two men arrived with him and shadowed the three gentlemen of the Caledonian Society wherever they went. Whether this was simple habit or some underhanded plan, nobody knew; but Dr. Graham spotted his tail and became incensed. He marched before Chief Carpenter and made everything very plain.

"I have authority from Premier Honoré Mercier himself to affect this meeting," he cried, red in the face and waving his cane. "And I demand that your men be called off immediately and that you do not interfere with us in any way. Do you understand?"

Chief Carpenter did not deny that the men were his detectives. He did his best to calm the good doctor, summoned his men and cursed them roundly for getting caught. He sent them back in disgrace to Marsden.

The search for Donald went on.

Easter Sunday

The day of resurrection was a day of uncommon rejoicing in the County of Compton in the year of 1889. Congregations in every church from Megantic Lake to Bishop's Crossing, from Red Mountain to Megantic Mountain, from the Chaudière to the Saint Francis, heard officially announced from their pulpits that a truce had been declared. All were asked to search for Donald and to inform him, if he were found, of a meeting scheduled for Monday morning in Winslow.

The Companions of the Iron Stove went hunting. Malcolm Matheson visited his camp. John Hall made enquiries around East Dudswell. The MacRitchie brothers took a walk up to Red Mountain. Colin Campbell went out to his cabin and the little French Canadian out to his barn. Dan and Bob MacDonald searched the North Hill. Mrs. Buchanan walked in the woods. The Matheson brothers, Willie and Pete, toured around Spring Hill. Murdo McArthur looked in his cellar. Mac McLean travelled the roads. Old Mrs. Campbell looked under her bed.

John McLeod borrowed a hand-car once more and pumped up the railway line hullooing into the woods.

"Donald Morrison! Huloo, Donald!"

But only the woods answered back.

Then Augusta's father visited his sugar camp and found the outlaw fast asleep on a bench.

He was dirty and haggard. He sported a week's growth of beard and was badly in need of a haircut but he grinned when he heard the news. He got up and went home.

Even the little rough cabin near Marsden could look like home to a man who had been denied one of any sort for ten long months. He arrived about seven in the evening. His father greeted him gruffly, as if he'd been gone just a few days, while his mother took one look and began preparing a good meal on the stove. What she had was plain enough but her son was home and safe at last and that seasoning made the poorest meal a feast.

Donald washed up and changed his clothes and talked with his father of the weather and the new spring coming. They spoke of harrowing and of planting and of breaking fresh land as soon as the ground permitted. Old Murdo became quite soft and sentimental.

"If the Lord spares me a few more years," he said, "I might just have a bit of a farm to be leaving you after all."

"Just be keeping yourself healthy," said Donald with a grin. "Don't be working yourself into an early grave."

"Early, you say?" The old man wheezed with pleasure. "I'll be seventy-seven in a few weeks, boy. Are you knowing that? Seventy-seven."

"I know that," said Donald and he also knew that his father was beyond breaking new land and building yet another farm. He might still manage a kitchen garden, but that would be the extent of his agriculture for he had faded rapidly in the past year. His skin was mottled with liver spots and his hands trembled and his eyes were pale as water. Donald sat down astride a chair to eat a bite of supper.

"We'll whup them yet, Donald, me boy," said the old man, completely lost in his pleasure. "They can't catch us, shoot us, drown us or starve us and we'll whup them yet. You'll see. A Lewis man, they say, goes in hard and keeps on going. Yes, sir! He does that and so he does!" He wheezed and chuckled again.

Donald told them of the proposed meeting with the representatives of the Caledonian Society and that he intended to give himself up. His father grew grave. His mother inspected the collar of his shirt to see it was clean and not frayed – no son of hers was going to jail with a dirty collar if she could help it. His father got out his Bible and his spectacles and laboriously went searching for a few comforting words he could carry along. His mother, far more practical, gave him a packet of biscuits and a small bottle of milk – and then she kissed him on the head – something she had not permitted herself since he was a lad of five or six.

Murdo accompanied him to the door, still searching rather desperately for inspirational luggage.

"Good night," said Donald. "I'll be seeing you both again just as soon as I'm able. Good night and take care now."

He stepped out into the darkness and was shot down.

Leroyer and McMahon

They suspected Donald might come to the cabin for his best clothes and they lay in ambush all day Saturday and most of Sunday. On Sunday evening they saw him enter and Leroyer crept to the window for a closer look. He saw Donald straddling a chair and eating his supper but thought he looked too old to be the man they hunted. McMahon came up for a look just as Donald's mother gave him the milk and the biscuits and knew him for sure. They drew back to a corner of the house and waited.

Donald came out.

"Up with your hands" roared McMahon.

Donald bolted. Both detectives fired their rifles at him and both missed, drew revolvers and raced after him firing as they ran. Donald kept going in spite of the hail of bullets and then dropped so suddenly that McMahon fell over him. Leroyer shoved his revolver in Donald's ear and ordered; "Keep your mouth shut or I blow your damn brains out!"

McMahon found Donald's pistols inside his coat wrapped up in a cloth to keep them from the damp and then jumped to intercept old Murdo who was hurrying from the cabin.

"Get back to the house," he roared. "Or I'll put a bullet through your head!"

The old man halted but he did not retreat. He watched

them pick his son up by the arms and the legs and he came two steps closer.

"Can you speak, Donald?"

"Yes," said Donald. He wasn't dead.

"Get back," yelled McMahon once more and they carried Donald some twenty yards to the top of a knoll. Leroyer ran off to bring help from the encampment. Murdock Murray, hearing the shooting from his house close by, came to see what had happened. Constables McKeown and Lessard, who had been stationed on the road a short distance from the cabin also in ambush, ran up to lend a hand. They wrapped Donald in a blanket and carried him to a house in the village and laid him face down on the floor. There was little blood. The bullet had entered his left buttock and emerged from his right hip. Donald made no moan.

Carpenter arrived to take charge. Peter Spanjaardt, never far behind the action, showed up a few minutes later. Donald was given brandy-and-sugar under all these eyes and made as comfortable as possible.

A special train was sent from Sherbrooke to pick him up. Donald was carried to the station on rugs and blankets.

While Sophie, his mother, broke down and wept and Murdo, his father, sat in his rocker and grimly stared at the wall . . . .

While Augusta brushed her dark hair in a Boston room and hummed of Colin's Cattle. . . .

While Dr. Graham became so upset at the news of his betrayal that he took to his bed and stayed there. . . .

While Judge Dugas deserted his guests and remained secluded in his study. . . .

While High Constable Bissonette poured himself another whisky and his wife pleaded with him to retire. . . .

While Spanjaardt toured the scene of the shooting, found blood spots on the cold ground, empty cartridge shells, McMahon's hat frozen in a puddle, a packet of biscuits and a small bottle of milk.

Part Three

Sherbrooke Courthouse

Dr. Graham recovered sufficiently to set up a "Morrison Defence Committee" with Hugh Leonard as Treasurer and Malcolm Matheson one of its most active supporters. By the time of the trial, they had collected over $2,000 and John Leonard, with this money, had hired two of the best trial attorneys in the land: Messrs. J. N. Greenshields and F. X. Lemieux. The prosecution was to be led by Charles Fitzpatrick, Deputy Attorney-General, and it was noted that these three – Greenshields, Lemieux and Fitzpatrick – had been the defence team for Louis Riel. Some took this as an indication that Donald had the very best. Others pointed out that Riel had been convicted and hanged.

Just before midnight on the eve of the trial, flames were spotted on the hilltop just north of Megantic. Duquette had tried hard to sell – the place being nothing but bad luck from the beginning – but could find no one willing to take the farm at any price. He had stocked the remaining barn with a summer's hay and it all went up in smoke that night. It was the very last of Donald's property.

Fierce, big-bearded, ham-handed Highlanders began drifting into Sherbrooke from the settlements. They spoke a strange language, kept to themselves and were curt and brusque with curious strangers. Old Murdo Morrison did not come. He claimed he had his potatoes to dig, but actually he lacked the money to be spending time in the city. Matheson understood his pride and did not offer charity. Malcolm B. McAulay came, but only because he was summoned as a witness, and repeatedly grumbled that he did not know why he had been brought into it at all for the trial had nothing to do with him. Reporters, lawyers, judges, police, detectives and hundreds of onlookers who had followed Donald's odyssey in the public press, filled the city streets and could talk of nothing else.

The trial began on October 1st, 1889. After five months in Sherbrooke Gaol, Donald was led into the prisoner's dock by the jailer and two uniformed constables. They were taking no chances. He leaned heavily on a cane and dragged his right leg but otherwise appeared cool, calm and in good health. Before Mr. Justice Brooks and Mr. Justice Wurtele, he was formally arraigned for the wilful murder of Lucius Warren on June 22nd, 1888.

He pleaded "Not guilty."

He was next arraigned on two counts of arson. The first in the burning of a barn belonging to M. Auguste Duquette on May 30th, 1888.

He pleaded "Not guilty."

The second in the burning of a house belonging to M. Auguste Duquette on May 30th, 1888.

He pleaded "Not guilty."

He was arraigned for shooting at James McMahon and Pierre Leroyer on April 21st, last, with intent to kill or maim.

He smiled bitterly and pleaded "Not guilty."

It was understood by almost everyone that conviction on the murder charge would result in all lesser charges being dropped and, likewise, all charges against the harbourers. Mac McLean was taken before a Grand Jury, just in case, and a true bill was brought against him for "having feloniously aided and harboured Donald Morrison against the Queen's writ and warrant" but few supposed he would ever actually face trial — let alone his seven companions. All hinged on the result of the murder charge.

The prosecution attempted to prove that Warren was shot and killed by the defendant while engaged in the lawful performance of his duty as a Special Constable. The defence did not deny that Donald had done the shooting but insisted that he had excellent reasons for believing Warren intended to kill him. They also maintained that the deputization was itself unlawful because Warren was not a British subject, not of good character and because the warrant was incorrectly filled out. Several character witnesses were brought forward, Malcolm Matheson foremost among them, and all testified that Donald was a man highly esteemed and respected in his community.

The trial lasted eight days. The jury was out for twenty-three hours. They returned with a verdict of "guilty of manslaughter" but hoped the judge would "give him the lightest penalty which you can conscientiously give."

That penalty lay entirely at the discretion of the court and could range from a fine of five cents to imprisonment for life. Most believed he would receive a term of two years. Some expected the recommendation of clemency to be disregarded in the face of Donald's long defiance of the law. Detective McMahon told reporters that even so, he did not believe Donald would receive a long sentence. Precedents were eagerly hunted out and discussed where men had received even less than two years for much harsher crimes.

On Friday, October 11th, the court reconvened to hear sentence passed.

The court was packed with spectators but all were dead silent.

"The sentence that this court pronounces on you is that you be confined to the Provincial Penitentiary at Saint Vincent de Paul at hard labour . . . for *eighteen years!*"

"Good God!" exclaimed the foreman of the jury. "We never expected that!"

Sherbrooke Gaol

Donald's lawyers immediately advised an appeal against the harshness of this sentence. The recommendation of clemency had been entirely ignored and the penalty reflected less the crime of manslaughter than that of resisting arrest, for which he had not been charged, but Donald flatly refused. It was over. His friends had already suffered far too much on his account and could be allowed to suffer no more. He could not put them through additional expense and additional trials. It was all over. He was less affected by the sentence than were his lawyers, for he had never expected justice, and though they begged and pleaded, he could not be moved. He thanked them all warmly for their efforts on his behalf and bade them a last goodbye.

Donald was transferred to the penitentiary. They shaved off his proud moustache and dressed him in a coarse grey prison uniform. They took away his name and gave him a number instead.

He was now number 2329.

St. Vincent de Paul Penitentiary

Eighteen years was a bleak long time and prison life was very hard on a man who had run free in woods and prairies for most of his days. It has been said that he was stubborn and determined but is it any wonder that his spirit failed him and he despaired in the end? He would be nearly fifty when he got out and too old then for a wife, a farm, a family. He decided to die.

He refused all food. He weakened steadily. Officials and friends attempted to argue him out of his resolve but he would have none of it. It was all over. He wanted it finished. Peter Spanjaardt was summoned to lend his weight to the appeals. He insulted Donald, called him a coward and a quitter, but Donald merely smiled and would not relent. He embraced consumption like a lover and failed visibly. Spanjaardt published his condition to the world and once again people flocked to his aid. Hundreds upon hundreds petitioned the Governor General for a pardon before it was too late.

But the wheels of the law move ponderously and are impersonal. The case was dusted off and examined. Details were discussed and discussed again. Political pressures were quite evident in the sentence, for it was Donald's long defiance of the powers of law and order with an accompanying threat to the entire judicial system of Quebec that had been held most against him. Mr. Justice Brooks had summed it up in his charge to the jury. "When a Queen's writ is issued," he had said, "that writ must be enforced, cost what it may, otherwise there is an end to all personal and social safety and order." Donald was imprisoned, then, less for the crime of manslaughter than for that of defiance.

On June 16th, 1894, when it became evident that Donald was dying and could no longer recover to threaten authority once more, the Minister of Justice signed a recommendation for his release. Peter Spanjaardt brought the news to the prison hospital. He found Donald pale, drawn and very weak, gasping for breath and coughing up blood. The Deputy Warden informed them that orders for his release were expected within three or four days and Donald whispered his thanks. If he could last that long, he might not have to die in prison after all.

He was released on the nineteenth of June and taken to the Royal Victoria Hospital around eleven in the morning. By then he could not speak and was hardly able to breathe. He died less than four hours later.

His estate, as reported by Spanjaardt, consisted of ten dollars given him by the penitentiary, another dollar contributed by an anonymous lady and a single penny of his own.

Gisla Cemetery

In a rosewood casket with a fine glass lid, Donald suffered through a brief service at the hospital and was then escorted by nearly two hundred mourners to Windsor Station and the train back to his beloved hills. He arrived at Marsden about four in the morning and was met at the station by Norman and Murdoch, his brothers. They loaded him aboard a buckboard and carried him to the little cemetery of Gisla.

There, surrounded by the woods and hills of home, Donald at last lay down to rest. There the people bade him a last *Soiridh!* – the friends and relatives who had sheltered him, his father, now eighty-two years old, who would lie beside him in less than a year, his mother, seventy-six, destined to go in hard and keep on going for twelve years yet, John Leonard, his friend and lawyer, and Augusta McIver still waiting for a question she would never hear.

Notes

The Scots

The Scots in this book were newcomers to Canada who had left their homes in the Highlands and Western Isles. Many of them had been "crofters." That is, they were tenants on very small farms and paid their rent in the form of a percentage of their produce. The land was not rich and their life was hard. But for countless generations they endured, tied to the soil by their own sweat and blood, as well as by an unbreakable spirit.

However, with the advent and growth of the Industrial Revolution, the British economy needed factory labourers, not small share-croppers. Secondly, the factories needed wool, supplied by vast flocks of sheep, and this could not be provided by tiny farms. Consequently, many of the traditional chiefs of the clans sold or leased the lands to the English. These new landlords wished to raise sheep on the land, and they systematically forced out the crofters. Sheep began to graze where men had worked.

Some people went to the city factories. But many refused to abandon their ties to the land. They emigrated. Companies cropped up to organize their colonization of the New World. For the most part the crofters were herded into boats whose destination they did not know.

Many settled in the Maritime Provinces, many in the prairies. A few ended up in the Eastern townships of Quebec.

Why did men like Murdo Morrison choose Quebec? There was better land in Nova Scotia and New Brunswick, but it was taken. There was richer land in Manitoba, but the journey was a crushing one. So, they chose Quebec. The land was rocky; it lent itself to forests, not farms; but it was land and it was theirs. No longer were they at the beck-and-call of a landlord. Their stubborn, unbending character, forged by generations of hardship, would break this land and bend it to their Scottish will.

The Scots in Megantic

By settling in Megantic, the Scots found themselves in a unique situation. On the one hand, in spite of the influx of English, Irish, and United Empire Loyalist immigration, Quebec society itself had changed little in a hundred years. The church occupied a dominant position. Indeed, it was not until 1854 that the seigniorial system (tenant farming on a nobleman's property) had been abolished. On the other hand, the Lewis Scots found themselves in a completely isolated and previously unsettled area. With their arrival in Megantic, the Eastern Townships had a new cultural heritage, religion, and set of values. The Scots formed a complete society. They could look for help only to themselves.

159

These settlers had left a landlord-run society where their presbyterian religion and Gaellic language had been repressed by English domination for several hundred years. This past struggle, combined with the fact that they now formed a new and physically isolated community, resulted in a unique situation.

What developed in communities like Megantic was a crusty, proud self-reliance. The settlers relied on each other and viewed the intruder with grave mistrust. Hence Monsieur Duquette could not have known the circumstances surrounding the sale of Donald's farm. Gradually this society of individualists developed an attitude against all outsiders including the representatives of law and authority from Montreal.

This was Donald's community. Its origins dictated that Donald be cherished and protected; that the spirit of the law, not the letter of the law, be revered; that the men of authority from Montreal be hoodwinked; that poor Monsieur Duquette receive no warning that he was unwittingly breaking the "code." This was Megantic in 1885.

Translations

Frontispiece: this is a stanza from a song of farewell to Scotland's Western Isles.

> "Farewell to each mountain and moor,
>   The mounts from which I must leave;
> Long may deer dwell in your hollows,
>   To be close to you will be my dream."

Page 23:
strupach – a cup of tea; in the Arctic it is a "mug-up"

Page 25:
ceilidh – a sing-song. These were frequent, major social events in rural Scotland.
Pibroch – a bag-pipe symphony. It is often played by two men. One plays his interpretation, then the other attempts to enhance it with variations. The exchange is considered a compliment and an honour.

Page 26:
> Ho ro, my nut-brown maiden,
>   Hi ri, my nut-brown maiden,
> My fair and lovely maiden,
>   I would marry only you.

Page 36:
This is a stanza from "Colin's Cattle," a very rhythmical melody, sung by milk-maids as they milked their cows.

> "Colin's cattle my beloved,
> Colin's cattle my dear;
> The cattle that will fill the pails,
> The cattle that will bear the çalves."

Page 46:
soirdh – farewell; good-bye

Page 74:
"Big mar tha sibh au neudh?" – How are you tonight?
"Gart tabihibh." – Fine thanks. Literally – "Like a row of standing corn."

Page 87:
"Tiomnadh – Nuadh" – New Testament.

Singing while they worked and played was an integral part of rural Scottish culture. Gaelic dialects varied from one area to another; this one has been corrupted in its move to the New World.

Comprehension

Pages 14-38

1. What were the steps that led to the Morrisons' loss of their farm?
2. How does the author use connotation in his descriptions of people to create character?
3. Describe Donald's skill with his guns. Why does the author illustrate Donald's ability in a humorous fashion?
4. What contribution does the sub-plot of Donald and Augusta make to the introduction of this story?

Pages 38-59

1. Illustrate how Major McAulay was "able to do just what he liked with the machinery of the law."
2. Why was M. Auguste Duquette the innocent victim of hostile surroundings?
3. Why was Major McAulay dissatisfied with the work of Constable Edwards?
4. What qualities did Jack Warren possess that made him an ideal constable in the Major's eyes?
5. How did Donald's killing of Jack Warren drastically change his position with the Law?

Pages 62-84

1. How did Donald's attendance at Warren's funeral contrast with the description of him on his arrest warrant?
2. What problems did Silas H. Carpenter encounter in his search for Donald?
3. What evidence is given to show that the French soldiers and the Scottish settlers now had a bond of communication?
4. What events are portrayed by the author that support Peter Spanjaardt's romantic description of Donald as "the Rob Roy of the region"?

5. How has the author made Chief Carpenter a rather sympathetic character in this section? Why is he portrayed in this way?

6. Why did Donald reject Chief Carpenter's offer?

Pages 85-106

1. How does the author continually suggest to us that Donald is doomed?

2. Why was Pierre Leroyer brought into the case?

3. How do Donald MacRitchie's reactions in the face of a crisis cast light onto Donald Morrison's character?

4. Trace the love affair of Donald and Augusta and explain its role in the story.

5. How did Donald's Gaelic tongue save his endangered neck at Mrs. Campbell's house?

6. Explain Chief Carpenter's statement, "that is the straw that broke the camel's back."

Pages 106-149

1. How did Judge Dugas attempt to change the community's protective attitude toward Donald?

2. How did the Scots react to Dugas' intimidating tactics?

3. What is the function of the chapter entitled "Mrs. Buchanan," pp. 117-118?

4. Outline the actions taken by Dugas to capture Donald prior to his meeting with the outlaw.

5. Was Donald justified in saying, "The law, sir, is a ass!" Explain your opinion.

6. What ironies can you see in Donald's being betrayed and ambushed on Easter Sunday?

Pages 152-157

1. What is symbolic in the burning of Duquette's barn?

2. Outline the charges against Donald and explain his plea to each charge.

3. What significance is seen in Donald's moustache being shaved?

4. What attitude do you think is revealed by the Ministry of Justice in recommending Donald's release?

Research and Writing

1. Investigate social and agricultural conditions in Scotland in the 18th century.

2. What were the effects of the Industrial Revolution on Scottish crofters in the mid-19th century? An excellent reference source for this is – James Prebble, *The Highland Clearances*, Penguin Books.

3. Research the "Ship Hector" and its effect on Nova Scotia from 1873 to 1900.
4. Where did the Scots settle in Canada? What were their hardships and their victories?
5. Who was Louis Riel? What role does he play in Canadian History? What contrasts and similarities exist between Louis Riel and Donald Morrison?
6. What is the ethnic make-up of the Eastern Townships of Quebec today? How is the situation today different from that of 1885?
7. Find and describe an historical situation in which a Canadian Indian or Eskimo was persecuted because of a too-rigid interpretation of the law.
8. How did the geography and social conditions of Lewis and Megantic shape the characters and attitudes of the Scots.
9. With the assistance of your teacher, obtain copies of some of Peter Spanjaardt's newspaper reports. Then write your own newspaper accounts of the Megantic outlaw.
10. Write an editorial in which you defend or deplore Donald's sentence.

Discussion and Debate

1. Language plays a vital role in our lives and in this story. Give examples, and explain the function of each of these types of language in the text:

   (a) legal language
   (b) ethnic language
   (c) emotional language
   (d) romantic language
   (e) ironic language

2. What are the problems today facing the immigrant to Canada whose native tongue is not English or French? What lessons can be learned from Donald's story?

3. Debate the following motion:

   "Be it resolved that because the Canadian system of government is based on the rule of law, that Donald Morrison should not have been protected, but should have been turned over to the Authorities."

4. How is the morality of Megantic in 1885 different from the morality of today? Which code of living is superior?

5. What are the qualities of a successful narrative? Assess the narrative worth of *The Outlaw of Megantic*.